Beyond the Ballot Box

Fairleigh Dickinson University Press Award

Beyond the Ballot Box (Dennis P. Ryan)

Beyond the Ballot Box

A Social History of the Boston Irish, 1845–1917

Dennis P. Ryan

Rutherford • Madison • Teaneck
Fairleigh Dickinson University Press
London and Toronto: Associated University Presses

Associated University Presses, Inc.
4 Cornwall Drive
East Brunswick, NJ 08816

Associated University Presses Ltd
27 Chancery Lane
London WC2A 1NF, England

Associated University Presses
2133 Royal Windsor Drive
Unit 1
Mississauga, Ontario, L5J 1K5, Canada

Library of Congress Cataloging in Publication Data

Ryan, Dennis P., 1943–
  Beyond the ballot box.

  Includes index.
  1. Irish Americans—Massachusetts—Boston—History.
2. Irish Americans—Massachusetts—Boston—Social
conditions.   3. Boston (Mass.)—History.   4. Boston
(Mass.)—Social conditions.   I. Title.
  F73.9.I6R9   1982   305.8'9162'074461   81-65874
  ISBN 0-8386-3116-9   AACR2

Printed in the United States of America

To the memory of my father,
who, in never missing Mass, a union meeting, or an op-
portunity to vote, showed me what it was and is to be
Irish, Catholic, and American. And to my mother, who
wisely loved him for doing so.

Contents

List of Illustrations

Fig 1. Autopsy report of Boston Irish cholera victim in 1849. (*Report of the Committee of Internal Health on the Asiatic Cholera* [Boston: 1849], p. 13. Courtesy of the Massachusetts State Library, State House, Boston)

Fig. 2. Saint Mary's Infant Asylum, an institution that cared for illegitimate infants, or those born of what one individual delicately called "unnatural parents." (Douglass S. Tucci, *The Second Settlement: A Study of Victorian Dorchester, 1875–1925* [Boston: 1974], page unnumbered.)

Fig. 3. Appointed Archbishop of Boston in 1907, William Henry Cardinal O'Connell (1859–1944) ruled the diocese with a firm hand for nearly four decades. (Courtesy of the *Boston Pilot*)

Fig. 4. Eye clinic of the Carney Hospital, founded in 1863 by the Irish philanthropist, Andrew Carney. (*Annual Report of the Carney Hospital for the Year 1898* [Boston: 1899], opposite p. 76. Courtesy of the Massachusetts State Library, State House, Boston)

Fig. 5. Irish maid, Annie Regan. (Courtesy of Helen Carroll)

Fig. 6. Monsignor Denis O'Callaghan (1841–1913), pastor of Saint Augustine's Parish for nearly fifty years, with graduates of the parochial high school. (Courtesy of the Sisters of Notre Dame de Namur Archives, Ipswich, Mass.)

Fig. 7. Surrounded by holy pictures, statues, and crucifixes, Irish students attending parochial schools were exposed constantly to the "lessons of piety and morality and reverence."

9

(Courtesy of the Archdiocese of Boston Archives, Brighton, Mass.)

Fig. 8. An illustration from an 1877 Boston parochial school textbook shows how some Irish Catholic children came to perceive the American Indian. (*Sadlier's Excelsior, Fifth Reader* [New York: 1877], inside cover page. Courtesy of the Monroe C. Gutman Library, Graduate School of Education, Harvard University, Cambridge, Mass.)

Fig. 9. Students at the middle-class Mount Saint Joseph Academy, around 1890. (Courtesy of the Archives of the Sisters of Saint Joseph, Brighton, Mass.)

Fig. 10. The O'Keeffe Grocery Store, Dorchester, around the turn of the century. The O'Keeffes later went into partnership with two other grocers to form what eventually became the First National Food Stores chain. (Douglass S. Tucci, *The Second Settlement: A Study of Victorian Dorchester, 1875–1925* [Boston: 1974], p. 64.)

Fig. 11. Irish immigrants learned early that Boston's streets were not paved with gold, but some, as contractors, found that fortunes could be made by digging them. Here workers in 1900 are building the East Boston Subway Tunnel. (*Sixth Annual Report of the Boston Transit Commission for the Year Ending August 15, 1900* [Boston: 1900], plate 4. Courtesy of the Massachusetts State Library, State House, Boston)

Fig. 12. Charles Logue (1858–1919), builder of Fenway Park, and family. (Courtesy of Robert J. Lawler)

Fig. 13. Like many Boston Irish attorneys, Congressman Henry F. Naphen (1852–1905) successfully divided his talents between public service and running a private law practice. (Courtesy of Special Collections, Boston College, Newton, Mass.)

Fig. 14. Michael Freebern Gavin (1844–1915), an eminent Boston Irish physician, in Civil War uniform. (*Michael Freebern Gavin, A Biography*, edited by his son [Cambridge, Mass.:

1915], opposite p. 16. Courtesy of the Francis A. Countway Library of Medicine, Boston Medical Library–Harvard Medical Library, Boston)

Fig. 15. Patrick Donahoe (1811–1901), publisher and editor of the "Irishman's Bible," the *Boston Pilot*, from 1839 to 1875. Note the crucifix around Donahoe's neck. (Courtesy of the *Boston Pilot*)

Fig. 16. The O'Connell family—a Boston Irish success story. Arriving as immigrants in the 1860s, Mr. and Mrs. James O'Connell had five sons, three of whom went on to become lawyers, another a veterinarian, and the youngest a well known sportswriter. (Courtesy of Lenahan O'Connell)

Fig. 17. Suspected by nativist Yankees of harboring Jesuit spies within their ranks and of serving as advance guards for the impending invasion of America by the Pope, Irish militia companies like the Columbian Artillery were forced to disband during the Know-Nothing hysteria of the 1850s. (*Gleason's Pictorial Companion*, vol. 3 (1852), p. 17. Courtesy of Massachusetts State Library, State House, Boston)

Fig. 18. John L. Sullivan (1858–1918), twelve years after he lost his heavyweight title, with baseball star Jimmy Collins. (Courtesy of the Boston Public Library)

Fig. 19. Politics, as this early 1900s handbill makes clear, was as much a form of entertainment for the Boston Irish as it was a vehicle to discuss issues. (Courtesy of the Holy Cross College Archives, Worcester, Mass.)

Fig. 20. Patrick J. Kennedy (second from left), a successful saloonkeeper, liquor dealer, politician, and grandfather of an American president, is shown here engaging in a card game with some friends. (Courtesy of John F. Kennedy Library, Dorchester, Mass.)

Fig. 21. John Boyle O'Reilly (1844–1890), poet, editor, and champion of racial and social justice. (Courtesy of the *Boston Pilot*)

Fig. 22. At parishes such as Saint Mary's in the North End, black Catholics worshiped alongside their Irish coreligionists. (*Golden Jubilee of the Society of Jesus in Boston, Mass., 1847–1897, St. Mary's Parish, Oct. 3, 4, 5 and 6, 1897* [Boston: 1897], p. 107. Courtesy of the *Boston Pilot*)

—Photography by Gregory Cecconi

Preface

The intention of this study, simply stated, is to investigate the nonpolitical experience of the Irish in Boston between 1845 and 1917. It examines their institutional and organizational response to poverty, their learning experience in the public and parochial schools, their difficulties in breaking into business and the professions, their relations with racial and ethnic groups other than Yankees, Irish women as domestics and in other roles, and finally, the Hibernians' leisure activities, which included militia companies, boxing, and, if it must be said, drinking establishments.

Unlike works that have traditionally focused on the rise of the Irish politically, this book should show us more comprehensively what life was like for the majority of Irish newcomers and help correct some long-standing misconceptions about them. A thorough look at their network of orphanages, asylums, and benevolent societies, for instance, refutes the contention made by some that the Irish were simply resigned to their earthly lot because of their adherence to the Catholic faith, which supposedly made them fatalistic and pessimistic.

The Irish were not, as one might think, of one mind where the merits of the public or the parochial school were concerned. At various times throughout the nineteenth century, they objected strenuously to the proselytizing influence endemic to the public school, perceived by some Yankee educators as a means of indoctrinating its predominantly Catholic immigrant students with Protestant American ways. Yet, despite these serious misgivings about the public school, the parochial school movement itself, for reasons far more complex than just financial difficulties, never took hold as firmly in

13

Boston as it did in other major urban Irish Catholic centers such as Chicago.

It is not easy to discern why the Boston Irish failed to climb the social ladder as rapidly as did later immigrant groups, most notably the Jews. Some place the onus on the parochial school, maintaining that it emphasized spiritual values over getting ahead, materially or occupationally. But the little green schoolhouse, or Irish Catholic parochial school, was as much concerned with achievement as was its rival, the little red schoolhouse, or public school. Therefore, we must look for other ways to explain why the sons of Erin, after nearly three generations, were by 1917 still concentrated in low-status, blue-collar jobs. Others try to explain the lack of social mobility by citing discrimination, evidenced by the "Help wanted: Irish need not apply" advertisements that sometimes appeared in Yankee newspapers. True, the Irish were to some degree victims of discrimination. Nonetheless, what ultimately hampered the Irish occupationally was not so much rabid discrimination as it was their misfortune—if that is the proper term—in succeeding too well in politics and the labor movement. A preoccupation with financial security can stifle an immigrant group's social aspirations. And the Boston Irish as a group were particularly shortsighted in opting for secure but financially dead-end jobs as government employees and union wage earners, rather than taking advantage of more remunerative and prestigious opportunities in business and the professions.

If the Boston Irish can be faulted in part for their lack of social mobility, they have not, on the other hand, received the appropriate recognition for their role in educating other immigrant and racial groups, such as the Jews, the Italians, and the blacks, in the intricacies and nuances of American life, especially as it pertained to politics and effective union organizing. At a critical time in our country's history, when some Americans were voicing serious doubts that the republic could survive as a racially and culturally pluralistic society, the Irish, in their daily give-and-take encounters with newer immigrants at the parish church, union hall, and caucus room, demonstrated that it could.

The experience of Irish women was different from that of all other immigrant women. Many arrived in Boston without husbands or families and consequently, out of economic necessity, entered domestic service. Overworked and poorly paid, stereotyped as being lazy, ignorant, and untrustworthy, the Irish maid heroically endured, managing not only to support herself but to send money back home. Other Irish women, as wives and mothers, saw to it that their families adapted to the vicissitudes of Boston immigrant life.

Leisure activities for the Irish represented more than a means of momentary escape from the cares and drudgeries of everyday life. Ostracized in many respects from the dominant, often hostile Yankee Protestant society, the Irish, reacting to discrimination and to an equally compelling desire to maintain their ethnic identity, socialized in their own parish churches, fraternal organizations, and neighborhood saloons.

This study terminates in 1917, when America entered World War I. At its conclusion, the Boston Irish found themselves the target of a different kind of nativism that profoundly affected their circumstances and institutions—a subject for a second volume.

Acknowledgments

Anyone attempting a study of this scope naturally incurs many debts of gratitude. My special thanks go to the University of Massachusetts for a research fellowship that helped this work progress during its dissertation phase, to Professor Milton Cantor of that institution for innumerable editorial and substantive suggestions, and to Amy Rebecca Kaufman for her stalwart editing. Joanne Laptewicz steadfastly typed parts of the manuscript; and my brother, John Francis Ryan, listened to me sympathetically throughout the six years spent writing this book and fortified me in a way that words cannot express.

Also deserving of special mention are Gregory Cecconi, photographer; Marie Murphy of the Boston Archdiocesan Office, Brighton, Mass.; Catharine Hayward of the Society of Saint Vincent de Paul, Boston; Father Joseph J. Shea, S.J., of the College of the Holy Cross, Worcester, Mass.; Professor David P. Twomey of Boston College; Thomas E. Cone, Jr., M.D., of the Children's Hospital Medical Center, Boston; Ronald K. West, proprietor of the Brady and Fallon Funeral Home; Robert J. Brink of the Social Law Library, Boston; Richard J. Wolfe, Curator of Rare Books and Manuscripts, Francis A. Countway Library of Medicine, Boston Medical Library-Harvard Medical Library, Boston; Robert W. Lovett, Curator of the Manuscript Division and Archives, Baker Library, Harvard University Graduate School of Business Administration, Boston; Albro Martin, Editor, Harvard *Business History Review;* Maurice Donahue, former president of the Massachusetts State Senate; Sister Jacqueline Glavin of the Sisters of Saint Joseph; the late Sister Dorothea Furfey of

17

the Sisters of Notre Dame de Namur; William J. Hourihan of Northeastern University; attorneys Edward B. Hanify, Lenahan O'Connell, and James A. Marsh; Thomas W. Kilmartin; John Cahill; Rosemary McEachern; Leo MacNeil; James Condon; James O'Toole, Archivist, Archdiocese of Boston, and his assistant, Kathleen McQuade; and the staffs of the Boston Public Library, the Massachusetts State Library (State House, Boston), and Saint John's Seminary Library, Brighton, Mass.

I thank the Boston Bar Journal for permission to reprint portions of my article, "The Rise of the Boston Irish Lawyer" (1979).

My deepest appreciation and gratitude are reserved for my mentor, the late Professor Howard H. Quint, of the University of Massachusetts. Mr. Quint, when I came to know him in the mid-1970s, was an anachronism in higher education. In an era when many dissertation chairmen were too absorbed in their own work to give adequate attention to their graduate students, Professor Quint, in striking contrast, gave unstintingly of his time, wisdom, and personal encouragement. He not only helped select two of the six topics discussed in this book but also scrutinized early drafts with uncommon meticulousness, offering criticisms, suggestions, and, when required, the solemn admonition to write more with my head than with my heart. For a second-generation Irish American like myself, this was no easy task, as Professor Quint well knew. I shall miss him as both teacher and friend.

Beyond the Ballot Box

1

The Irish Against Poverty

Go among the poor yourself, see for yourself, no
tongue can tell you one tenth part of what you will
realize when you see . . . the point of the nails and
put your finger into the place of the nails that have
fastened so many a poor man and woman living in
anguish crucified on the cross of poverty.

Thomas F. Ring, letter dated November 1891

To the thousands of Irish immigrants who passed through
Boston's port during the 1840s, the city signified a hopeful, if
apprehensive, beginning. Bewildered and frightened, the
newcomers could at least take comfort in the fact that they had
escaped the fate of more than half a million of their countrymen who perished during the potato famine. Having made the
desperate choice between the ship and the coffin, they were
convinced that the worst was behind them, for nothing could
have been as hopeless as to remain in Ireland, a country that
one poet lamented as "a land without stars." Yet the hardships
of the recent past would continue to haunt the Irish in their
new surroundings.[1]

Unskilled laborers from rural backgrounds, the Irish were
misfits in Boston's urban and commercial setting, where a
special skill or trade was necessary in order to earn a living. In
addition, the discrimination reflected in newspaper employment advertisements specifying that "None need apply but
Americans" prevented them from procuring decent jobs, and
they were condemned to live in miserable slums located in the

21

ELLEN McCANN. *Aged* 19. *Domestic. Irish. Tem-*
*perate. Cholera for ten hours. In Hospital four
hours. Treatment—" Saline mixture" every half
hour. Autopsy 20 hours after death.*

Rigor mortis sufficient. Some lividity of finger
nails; not much elsewhere. Abdomen natural in
shape.

Spinal cord (examined first) every way natural. A
drachm or two of clear serum in cavity of sheath,
which collects at bottom of cord. Sheath and arachnoid quite pale and healthy looking. Cord has a
natural degree of vascularity, and its substance is
everywhere of proper color and consistence.

Head. Dura-mater and arachnoid natural. Bloody
fluid, as before, just sufficient to smear posterior part of
hemispheres. Color of brain natural; consistence
firm. Ventricles contain little or no fluid; lining
membrane pale. Medulla oblongata also natural.

Chest. No dryness of pleura in front, but a very
little on diaphragmatic surface of right lung. Pericar-
dium natural internally; no ecchymoses; contains a
about half a drachm of clear serum. Right cavities
of heart filled with dark, fluid, rather thickish blood,
with trifling, soft coagula. Adjacent veins contain
same. Left ventricle tolerably firm; contains, with
auricle, a moderate quantity of dark fluid blood.

Heart natural internally; no staining.

Aorta contains much dark fluid blood, absolutely
without coagula.

Both lungs crepitate well everywhere, and are of a
natural red color externally and internally. There
are some dark patches on the posterior surface of
right, like those described in the case of *Ellen Keith,*

13

Fig. 1. Autopsy report of Boston Irish cholera victim in 1849.

South Cove and Fort Hill sections of the city. Officials declared that they posed a threat to the community's social fabric and drained the public treasury and the resources of Yankee benevolent societies. Immigrants accounted for 97 percent of the residents at the Deer Island almshouse, 75 percent of the prisoners in the county jail, 90 percent of Boston's truants and vagabonds, and 58 percent of its paupers.[2]

In the cellars of converted warehouses and buildings, where the backwater of Boston Harbor often inundated their pitiful living quarters, the Irish, "huddled together like brutes," were easy prey for the cholera epidemic of 1849, in which 509 of them perished. An old gunhouse was converted into a hospital, and Yankee physicians bravely visited patients in the notorious Half Moon Place, where they searched, among fever-ravaged faces reflecting a "listless indifference to their fate," for those who could still be helped. One man's hovel was a floating tomb: while ministering to a patient whose bed was surrounded by water, a doctor observed the coffin of an infant sailing about the room.[3]

The Irish soon began to take the initiative against poverty. Progress was slow at first. The Charitable Irish Society contributed money—but the 175 dollars distributed in 1849 did little to ease the suffering. More effective in aiding newcomers was the Irish Emigrant Society, founded in 1850, whose agent, Edward Ryan, helped immigrants find temporary employment, locate lost relatives, or make transportation arrangements out West, where there was plenty of cheap land and steady work building railroads and canals. Overseeing the movement of thousands, Ryan was always on guard against "land sharks" plotting to fleece unsuspecting immigrants. Some of these scoundrels were themselves Irish, or "Harpies," as the *Boston Pilot*, a Catholic weekly, contemptuously called them. Following the custom of their cohorts in other port cities, they were likely to sport bright green neckties and warm smiles. After winning the confidence of their latest victims, they would steer them to a waterfront saloon or boardinghouse where the proprietor, working in collusion and talking of "the ould counthry," would bilk them.[4]

Over the centuries, the Catholic Church, both in Ireland and on the Continent, had developed a system of orphanages, asylums, and hospitals, staffed by religious orders that later adapted these institutions to meet American conditions—a cultural transplant of great benefit to Boston's Irish immigrants. As early as 1833, the Sisters of Charity had established the Saint Vincent Female Orphan Asylum, which cared for children who had lost both parents during the cholera epidemic. Directed by Sister Ann Alexis, a woman of "rare executive ability," the Asylum, supported in part by generous contributions from Yankee Protestants, was providing for more than 300 youngsters by the 1860s. The Home for Destitute Catholic Children, founded in 1864, was governed by a board of laymen that included Patrick Donahoe, editor of the *Pilot*, and Charles Francis Donnelly, a prominent attorney from County Roscommon, who insisted that the Home be a temporary resting place for children who eventually were to be returned to their natural parents or released for adoption. One father who asked that three of his children be taken in was rejected by Superintendent Bernard Cullen on the grounds that he was a "stout able man" and the reputed owner of two houses. Cullen only admitted children who were abandoned or neglected or whose parents were unable to support them. In 1869 he admitted a six-year-old girl whose mother had recently died "in a fit of intoxication" and whose father was reportedly "pursuing the same course." Cullen rescued the children of a "habitual drinker" who had broken his "wife's breast bone and then deserted" his family and provided shelter for a four-year-old boy whose father was serving a prison term for murdering his wife. Parents, often drunk, threatened to break Cullen's nose or "overhaul" him physically.[5]

Before releasing a child for adoption, Cullen usually obtained character references on prospective parents from the parish priest, postman, or police officer. After receiving custody of a child, foster parents were required to submit regular reports regarding his schooling and church attendance, and Cullen himself frequently checked on the child's adjustment to his new environment. If unable to find suitable foster homes in New England, he would travel across the nation in his search. Yet even the best of intentions did not always guarantee a satisfactory placement. Children were sometimes returned for being incorrigible, "saucy," or "not good natured enough." Exploitation of the children as domestics or laborers was not uncommon. One youngster claimed her adoptive guardian "persecuted her for being a Catholic"; another complained of "being perverted by a Methodist woman with whom she lived."[6]

Receiving on probation "intractable" Catholic children who had appeared before municipal court judges, Cullen usually referred the boys to the House of the Angel Guardian in the North End. Founded in 1851 by Father George Foxcroft Haskins, a Harvard College graduate and former Episcopalian minister who had converted to Catholicism, the home was to be a "moral restaurant," or "temporary" resting place "on the great thoroughfare of life." Long-term confinement was considered detrimental to the youth's development because he could fall into a routine "fatal to all ambition and elevation of character, and virtue, and religion." Parents and guardians committing their boys to the home were asked to pay a token fee, which, according to Haskins, "gave them a certain sense of wholesome independence to reflect that they were able to pay something for their children's keeping and teaching." The youth, in turn, would come into the home "with something of the pride of the lad who starts for college." By 1899 the home had attempted to rescue more than 10,000 boys from the "seething cauldron of pauperism or of crime." Haskins viewed corporal punishment as "a relic of barbarism, degrading alike to the child and the teacher," and employed a disciplinary system that was "mild and persuasive, though strict." Upon completion of their religious and common school training, the boys were usually apprenticed to farmers, bootmakers, and tailors.[7]

The House of the Good Shepherd, administered by the Sisters of the Good Shepherd, provided shelter for girls and women troubled by habitual drunkenness and lives "of sin and misery." As "a refuge from temptation and a sanctuary of sweetness," the Sisters tried to "reclaim the thoughtless and melt the hardened," who were segregated into three classes, each receiving special guidance: the Preservates, the Penitents, and the Magdalens. The Preservates, girls between nine and eighteen years of age who had been "badly brought up" or "exposed to great moral danger," received a grammar school education and were trained in general housekeeping, embroidery, and needlework. The Penitents, mostly women who had entered the home voluntarily, dramatized their break with a sinful past by discarding their former names and assuming saintly ones. Struggling for religious regeneration through incessant work and prayer, some stayed for years; others, having "regained will-power," returned quickly to society, "safe, useful and virtuous." For the third group, the Magdalens, the outside world was permanently closed off. These former Penitents chose to consecrate themselves to a life of contemplation and prayer. Forming their own religious community, the Magdalens took separate vows and wore a special brown habit but were not permitted to become sisters in the order of the Good Shepherd—to belong to this particular order, a woman had to possess a "spotless character" and come from a family of "blameless reputation."[8]

Infants born illegitimate, or of "unnatural parents," as one individual delicately called them, were an additional problem for the Boston Irish. The Carney Hospital, founded in 1863 by Andrew Carney, a wealthy Irish merchant and property owner, set aside a ward for abandoned infants and unwed mothers in 1870. This arrangement infuriated Carney's widow. She withheld from the hospital part of her late husband's promised financial support and had his remains removed from the hospital burial grounds. In response, Boston Archbishop John J. Williams purchased a twelve-acre estate overlooking Dorchester Bay for the Saint Mary's Infant Asylum. From the beginning, the Asylum was plagued by a high mortality rate. Competent institutional child care hardly existed, and babies placed in foundling asylums instead of foster homes were almost inevitably doomed to early deaths—

Fig. 2. Saint Mary's Infant Asylum, an institution that cared for illegitimate infants, or those born of what one individual delicately called "unnatural parents."

children at Saint Mary's "all died with few exceptions." The infant mortality rate, thought by some to be 97 percent, especially concerned the Society for the Prevention of Cruelty to Children, a non-denominational agency that sympathized with the Catholics' desire to care for their own. Still, the Society threatened to turn over to state institutions Catholic infants coming under its jurisdiction, unless drastic improvements were made at the Asylum. A nun who visited the institution in the winter of 1893 wrote, "We found about 60 of the most forlorn children I ever saw. It seemed to me every one had sore heads, sore ears, and very weak and sore eyes."[9]

These conditions were compounded by financial mismanagement and constant feuding between the sisters who resided at the Asylum and the home's board of directors, consisting of a diocesan priest and laymen. A serious argument revolved around the Asylum's $70,000 mortgage. For their own protection, the sisters desired a corporation charter that would explicitly make the Archbishop of Boston, rather than their own religious order, liable for all debts incurred by the Asylum. Frequently, the sisters threatened to abandon Saint Mary's, and on one occasion they did. The Asylum would surely have closed during these turbulent years had it not been for John O'Brien, who negotiated an agreement which guaranteed the sisters full control over the internal affairs of Saint Mary's, while the Archbishop, in turn, accepted overall responsibility for the institution's administration and debts.[10]

Between 1859 and 1864, an average of 27 Irish women were sentenced each year to the Deer Island House of Industry for being "Common Night Walkers." Ranging in age from 15 to 47, most were single and illiterate. Bernard Cullen, the Catholic court agent, was on guard against this problem. In 1870 the police chief summoned him to the station to question 103 suspects arrested during a raid on the city's red-light district. Of these, Cullen was relieved to find that only 14 were his "own people." And all but one of those convicted for keeping a house of ill fame, he boasted, "were non-Catholic." In the winter of 1895 it was reported that "women, flashily dressed," were trying to recruit Irish immigrant girls as prostitutes at the East Boston docks, and the Charitable Irish and Saint Vincent de Paul Societies quickly investigated. Over the next five months, Miss Nellie McGurty, a special agent who greeted and counseled more than two thousand females debarking at East Boston, found not "a trace of the abuse hinted at." For the most part, the girls had prepaid tickets and were met at the wharfs by friends and relatives.[11]

To accommodate the hundreds of homeless bootblacks and newspaper boys, Father David H. Roche in 1883 founded the Working Boys' Home in the North End. To help sustain itself, the institution published its own monthly magazine, *The Working Boy*, and formed a musical band that performed at various social functions throughout the Irish community; and in 1888 the boys, who had been taught the values of self-help, hard work, and sobriety, organized their own temperance society. Three square meals a day, a recreation room, a library, and white-sheeted, warm beds all helped to save the boys from the moral pitfalls of Boston after dark. The Working Girls' Home, located off Harrison Avenue, a South End street lined with other protective and charitable institutions, surrounded Irish domestics and factory workers with "refining influences" and taught them how to "work, to gain more wages, to get independent." The girls were free to come and go as they wished, and attendance at Sunday Mass was voluntary. Most of the girls found all the rest and recreation they needed either in "their cosy rooms or in the companionship of one another in the cheery alcoves."[12]

Individual Irish charity workers likened their role to that of "gleaners following after the reapers, finding here and there a few stalks of grain overlooked by the workmen." Most volunteers belonged to the Society of Saint Vincent de Paul, which was organized by conferences at the parish level. Providing the "Vincentian" with the opportunity for self-sanctification through acts of mercy, the Society offered temporary assistance to the poor, usually in the form of food, shelter, or clothing. Some members did more: in 1886, when the neighbors of a dead woman refused to make burial arrangements, one Vincentian built a casket and "performed all the duties of an undertaker." One of the Society's fundamental principles was that intimate contact with the needy was essential to a deep understanding of poverty. "By a friendly visit," wrote Thomas F. Ring, the Society's president, "the poor man feels that he is not alone in the world, he has someone to whom he can relieve his mind by speaking of his troubles and misfortunes." Gaining the confidence of those he visited, the Vincentian was in a position to offer friendly advice regarding employment and the religious upbringing of children. Like Protestant benevolent societies, the Society was careful to avoid fostering social parasites. Assistance was offered only after thorough investigation, and cash payments were discouraged because they tended to result in the "demoralization of the poor." Even the distribution of turkeys at Christmastime was monitored closely lest they be sold by recipients for cash. One North End conference insisted that the poor keep clean houses as a prerequisite for relief; another issued food coupons redeemable only at grocery stores that did not sell alcoholic beverages.[13]

The Society's president had as little patience for the seller of liquor as he did for the consumer. It was incongruous to him to admit saloonkeepers to a "society which has to repair so much trouble arising from the intemperate use of liquor." Ring also fought against the admission of women, feeling they would only "create confusion and sow dissatisfaction." His troubles were compounded by the difficulty in recruiting young men, which led many to view the organization as an "old man's society," by the tendency of some conferences to discontinue their services during the humid summer months, and by parish priests' extravagant almsgiving practices, which in one instance so embarrassed the Society that Ring threatened to cut off assistance.[14]

In the 1880s, salaried charity officials and trained social workers began to replace volunteers, and Ring acknowledged this progress by employing an agent to handle the backlog of children's cases pouring into the Society's Charity Building office. Addressing a national conference of nondenominational charity workers in New Haven in 1895, Ring asserted that the professional was "a more judicious and wiser helper than the average volunteer visitor, whose zeal is greater than his experience." But the Irish were wary of "charity expressmen," or paid experts who went about collecting sociological and statistical data on the poor, an activity that could only lead to what one parish priest labeled "red tape-ism." He remarked, "Do you suppose I would permit the names of those of my people in need to be card-catalogued and kept on record with all the details of their family life and connections?"[15]

Catholic children confined to state institutions complained of Protestant chaplains "snapping up" or burning their catechisms. In dealing with non-Catholics, Ring advised Vincentians "to cultivate friendly relations, be pleasant, and as far as you can do it, be obliging and ready to do a favor," but he warned against "entangling alliances." The Children's Aid Society was considered the "most proselytizing" Protestant agency in Boston and was distrusted by Ring, who found its president "to be a fair spoken man who talks turkey and gives us crow."[16]

William Henry O'Connell's accession to the archbishopric of Boston in 1907 marked a new era in the history of Catholic charity organizations. Vain and pompous, O'Connell's dynamic leadership brought order to the innumerable charities that had come into being during the previous half-century under his predecessors, Bishop John Bernard Fitzpatrick and Archbishop John Williams. Like a clerical Bismarck, he imposed his ecclesiastical authority upon those Catholic superintendents and managers who insisted upon running their institutions like private estates.[17]

Born of Irish parents in Lowell, Massachusetts, in 1859, the youngest of eleven children, O'Connell attended the city's public schools, where he was subject to frequent ethnic and religious slurs. He entered Saint Charles' Seminary in Maryland in 1876 but withdrew after two years because of bad health. He completed his education at Boston College, finishing first in his class. Re-entering the seminary, his studies took him to Rome, and in 1884 he was ordained a priest. As a curate at Saint Joseph's Church in Boston's West End, he mingled with impoverished Italians, "darkies," and hundreds of Irish. Gaining a quick reputation as an "eloquent and popular priest," O'Connell in 1895 was awarded the prestigious position of Rector of the North American College in Rome. O'Connell loved the city's antiquity, culture, and clerical intrigues and especially cherished the Church's tradition of papal authority. He applied himself diligently and, upon completion of his duties in the Eternal City, refined his administrative skills as Bishop of Portland, Maine, and then as papal envoy to Japan. Known in some circles as the "bishop without white hair" because of his rapid rise within the Church hierarchy, O'Connell returned to Boston in 1906 as assistant to the aging Archbishop Williams.[18]

When he became Archbishop of Boston, O'Connell immediately set out to improve the archdiocese's "very precarious moral and financial condition" by introducing "genuine

Fig. 3. Appointed Archbishop of Boston in 1907, William Henry Cardinal O'Connell (1859–1944) ruled the diocese with a firm hand for nearly four decades.

business management" procedures. In 1907 he appointed the first director of the Catholic Charitable Bureau, who provided him with detailed information: how each charitable institution was governed, the number of inmates, the amount of debts, mortgages, and annual receipts. (In his first year in office O'Connell generated more official correspondence than Williams, his predecessor, had done in his entire forty-one-year tenure.) In 1908, recognizing the critical need for a greater exchange of ideas and information between the splintered Catholic social agencies, he convened the first diocesan conference of Catholic charities. He purchased the *Pilot* in 1908 and through its weekly columns helped to raise, over a ten-day period, the astonishing sum of $250,000 for a hospital project.[19]

The chubby-faced prelate gave his attention to the smallest of details. In 1909, for example, he demanded that one of the trustees of a home for unwed mothers explain why board meetings were not held at the institution and, apparently for his own convenience, in the evenings. The trustee informed O'Connell that evening meetings tended to run late and that the sight of men leaving a maternity hospital under the cover of darkness "might be a cause of comment by some evil disposed persons." O'Connell got the point, but his will prevailed. On another occasion, a hospital official requested funds for a sun parlor to help "keep down the death rate." Though sympathetic, O'Connell rejected the request as "a matter of dollars and cents." "It is better to wait until you have sufficient funds," he warned, "because an accumulation of debts always results in disaster." Hearing rumors in 1908 that the Carney Hospital was suffering from mismanagement that could possibly embarrass the Church, he requested a financial statement from the hospital officials. Assured that the institution was solvent, he nonetheless cautioned against incurring new debts before old ones were paid, pointing out that "the way must be clear and Pelion must not be piled upon Ossa."[20]

A major source of irritation to O'Connell was the Working Boys' industrial training school in Newton Highlands, burdened with a $65,000 mortgage and constant feuding between

the superintendent—Father James Redican, a diocesan clergy-
man—and its religious brothers. Charges and countercharges
of mismanagement were bitterly exchanged. The brothers insisted upon taking orders only from their Superior General
stationed in Belgium, and one of them accused Redican of
usurping their authority and making them "entirely pow-
erless." The brothers, in turn, were charged not only with
dereliction of duty but with sexual abuse of the boys. One
brother had been expelled, reported a diocesan priest, for "im-
moral practices with boys in the infirmary"; another had been
accused openly by the inmates of "indecently suggestive conversation." With characteristic vigor, O'Connell relieved the
brothers of their duties, brought in a new religious community to administer the internal affairs of the school, and appointed as trustees a group of laymen to oversee the general
management of the institution.[21]

On major social questions such as intemperance, O'Connell, like most of the Church's hierarchy, favored moral sua-
sion. He cautioned organizations like the Catholic Total Abstinence Union of America against resorting to the hatchet-
swinging, bar-smashing tactics of the temperance fanatic. On
issues involving management and labor, he favored voluntary
arbitration, reminding employers of their moral obligation to
provide for the welfare of their employees and repeatedly cau-
tioning union leaders against imprudent strikes and excessive
wage demands. With regard to state involvement in education, O'Connell warned against the threat of "over-legislation"
and "exaggerated organization." Believing that the Church
and parents, rather than the state, knew what was best for
children, he strenuously opposed government efforts to prohibit the employment of minors in factories. He also rebuked
the secular trend of replacing Christian charity with "scientific
charity." A society's efforts "to turn over its human problems
to the professional social worker trained along purely mathematical lines" might produce impressive reports, he warned,
"but they don't solve social problems."[22]

Certain clergymen within both Protestant and Catholic
churches challenged O'Connell's philosophy and insisted that

church leaders take a more active role in fighting for social justice. These so-called Social Gospelers criticized the fatalistic attitude that "the poor ye shall always have with you." During the 1880s, Protestant ministers at Andover Seminary and the Harvard Divinity School were searching for a more modern and applied Christianity through the study of sociology, social statistics, and political economics. Poverty, students learned, was not divinely ordained but socially created, and they insisted on greater Church support of state intervention in defending the rights of workers and improving the living conditions of the poor.[23]

None of this intellectual inquiry was tolerated at O'Connell's diocesan seminary. Since its opening in 1884, the faculty at Saint John's Seminary had been dominated by the Sulpician Fathers, a French order. The Archbishop's experience as a young man at the Sulpician-administered Saint Charles' Seminary in Maryland had been unpleasant, and, as the diocese's chief prelate, he was anxious to exercise his prerogative to appoint the priests of his choice at the seminary, especially now that American-born priests were becoming available. O'Connell also felt that the Sulpicians had plotted against his appointment as Williams's assistant in 1906, and their sympathy with the liberal social philosophy of Cardinal James Gibbons and Archbishops John Ireland and John J. Keane was distasteful to him. In O'Connell's opinion, a religious order that looked to France or to the Catholic University of America rather than to conservative Rome was unfit to serve as mentor to Boston's future priests. In 1910, in a meeting with the Sulpicians' Superior General, O'Connell accused the Sulpicians of being involved in a national plot to form "coteries and cliques against the bishops, especially with regard to their governing of the seminaries," and singled out Father Francis Havey, the Rector at Saint John's, for special criticism. Havey was alleged to have said that "the Roman system was worth nothing." Shortly thereafter, the Sulpicians left the Brighton seminary and were replaced by diocesan priests. Relying on an outmoded curriculum that emphasized Sacred Scripture, Church History, Canon Law, and dogmatic theology, Saint John's Seminary produced no social critic of the stature of Father John A. Ryan of Minnesota, a leading Catholic advocate of the Social Gospel.[24]

Believing the best kind of help was self-help, the Boston Irish, under the leadership of O'Connell, who was elevated to Cardinal in 1911, built an impressive network of social agen-

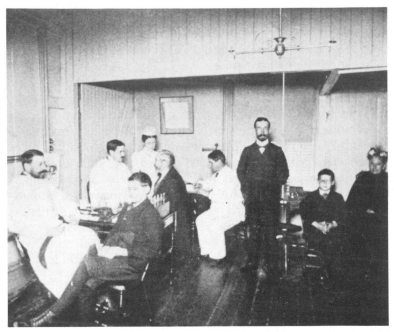

Fig. 4. Eye clinic of the Carney Hospital, founded in 1863 by the Irish philanthropist, Andrew Carney.

cies and charitable institutions and by 1917 were caring for approximately fourteen thousand of their sick and poor. Reflecting the Catholic Church's long tradition of pastoral care and the generosity of prominent laymen like Andrew Carney, Thomas Ring, and Patrick Donahoe, as well as that of thousands of working-class people, these institutions also provided an alternative to public institutions where Protestant missionaries were known to have wandered through corridors looking for converts and where, contrary to Catholic teaching, soup containing meat was offered to patients on Fridays. To the Boston Irish, Catholic-run institutions provided physical as well as spiritual refuge. Leading non-Catholic Boston social workers would recognize this world of ethnic and religious kinship but, as outsiders, would never fully understand it.[25]

NOTES

1. Oscar Handlin, *Boston's Immigrants, A Study in Acculturation*, rev. and enl. ed. (Cambridge, Mass.: 1959), pp. 39–52; quote in Dennis Clark, *The Irish in Philadelphia, Ten Generations of Urban Experience* (Philadelphia: 1973), p. 5, 24, 25. For further information on the famine years and immigration see R. Dudley Edwards and T. Desmond Williams, eds., *The Great Famine: Studies in Irish History, 1845–52* (New York: 1957); Cecil Woodham-Smith, *The Great Hunger: Ireland 1845–1849* (New York: 1962); Terry Coleman, *Going to America* (New York: 1972); Philip Taylor, *The Distant Magnet: European Emigration to the U.S.A.* (New York: 1971); and Oscar Handlin, *The Uprooted* (Boston: 1951).

2. Handlin, *Boston's Immigrants*, pp. 55–62, 68, 93, 100, 104–16; Massachusetts Sanitary Commissioners, *Report of a General Plan for the Promotion of Public and Personal Health* (Boston: 1850), pp. 200–204.

3. Handlin, *Boston's Immigrants*, pp. 114, 115; Barbara Gutmann Rosenkrantz, *Public Health and the State: Changing Views in Massachusetts, 1842–1936* (Cambridge, Mass.: 1972), pp. 30–32; *Report of the Committee of Internal Health on the Asiatic Cholera* (Boston: 1849), pp. 12–15, 172–73, 175, 180, deposited in Massachusetts State Library, State House, Boston.

4. *The Records of the Charitable Irish Society, No. 3*, 17 March and 17 December, 1849, Massachusetts Historical Society, Boston; Robert H. Lord, John E. Sexton, and Edward T. Harrington, *History of the Archdiocese of Boston* (New York: 1944), 3 vols., 2:455–57; *Boston Pilot*, 13 July, 4 May, 1 June, and 9 March 1850, 27 September 1856, 1 July 1854, 6 August 1853, 21 April 1855; Robert Ernst, *Immigrant Life in New York City, 1825–1863* (New York: 1949), pp. 27, 28. For Yankee efforts to combat poverty see George Silsbee Hale, "The Charities of Boston and Contributions to the Distressed of Other Parts," in *The Memorial History of Boston, 1630–1880*, ed. Justin Winsor, 4 vols. (Boston: 1880–81), 4:641–74; Nathan I. Huggins, *Protestants Against Poverty: Boston's Charities, 1870–1900* (Westport, Conn.: 1971).

5. Handlin, *Boston's Immigrants*, p. 162; Lord, Sexton, and Harrington, *History of the Archdiocese*, 2:629–32, 635–38; 3:361, 362, 391; *Boston Pilot*, 27 March 1875, 14 December and 26 October 1850; *Boston Republic*, 8 April 1882; *Fourth Annual Report of the Association for the Protection of Destitute Roman Catholic Children in Boston* (Boston: 1868), pp. 1–9; *XV and XVI Annual Reports of the Association for the Protection of Destitute*

Roman Catholic Children in Boston from Jan. 10, 1879 to Jan. 13, 1881 (Boston: 1881), pp. 6, 7, Massachusetts State Library, State House, Boston; Journal of the Superintendent of the Home for Destitute Catholic Children, 27 October 1866, 6 October 1869, 14 June 1868, 1 April 1870, 7 June 1867, Nazareth Child Care Center, Jamaica Plain, Mass. (hereafter cited as Superintendent's Journal).

6. *Statement of the Work of the Home for Destitute Catholic Children* (Boston: 1889), pp. 22–25, 26, 29, 30; Superintendent's Journal, 8 February 1867, 1 February 1871, 27 October 1870, 13 July, 17 August, 2 September 1871, 24 January 1867, 9 July 1869; *Thirteenth Annual Report of the Association for the Protection of Destitute Roman Catholic Children in Boston* (Boston: 1878), p. 11.

7. Lord, Sexton, and Harrington, *History of the Archdiocese*, 2:267, 268, 632–35; *The Life of Father Haskins by a Friend of the House of the Angel Guardian* (William Kelly) (Boston: 1899), pp. 69, 78, 114, 115, 151; Rev. George F. Haskins, *House of the Angel Guardian Report* (Boston: 1870), pp. 10, 14; Haskins, *House of the Angel Guardian Report for the Year Ending May 31, 1852* (Boston: 1852), pp. 16, 17; *House of the Angel Guardian Report* (Boston: 1868), p. 31 (reports deposited at the Massachusetts State Library, State House, Boston).

8. Lord, Sexton, and Harrington, *History of the Archdiocese*, 3:372–75; *The Work of the Good Shepherd in Boston* (Boston: 1872?), pp. 5–7; *Boston Pilot*, 29 January 1910; *Second Report of the Good Shepherd* (Boston: n.d.); *Boston Republic*, 17 June 1886, 2 May 1896.

9. Letter dated November 18, 1893, Thomas F. Ring Papers, deposited at the Boston office of the Society of Saint Vincent de Paul; Lord, Sexton, and Harrington, *History of the Archdiocese*, 2:638; 3:362–64; David Fitzgerald, *Carney Hospital, Boston, One Hundredth Anniversary, 1863–1963* (Boston: 1963?), pages unnumbered. Between 1875 and 1880 alone, an estimated 4 percent of Irish births in Boston were out of wedlock (Elizabeth Hafkin Pleck, *Black Migration and Poverty, Boston 1865–1900* [New York: 1979], p. 164); George B. Mangold, *Problems of Child Welfare* (New York: 1920), pp. 436, 470; Ring to his cousin, undated; Ring to Reverend Peter Ronan, 15 March 1897, Ring Papers; Sister Mary Edmund, "Historical Sketch: St. Mary's Infant Asylum and Lying-In-Hospital, St. Margaret's Hospital, Dorchester," manuscript, 1974, St. Margaret's Hospital, Dorchester, Mass.; John O'Brien, "The Early History of St. Mary's Asylum and Lying-In-Hospital," pp. 19, 20, manuscript, 1920, St. Margaret's Hospital.

10. Lord, Sexton, and Harrington, *History of the Archdiocese*, 3:363, 364; O'Brien, "The Early History of St. Mary's Asylum and Lying-In-Hospital," pp. 5–8, 11–14, 19, 20; Edmund, "St. Mary's Infant Asylum," pp. 13, 14, 28.

11. *Register, House of Industry, Deer Island, January, 1858–May, 1865*, deposited at Deer Island House of Correction, Boston; Superintendent's Journal, 8 and 9 May 1870; *Report of the Joint Committee of the Charitable Irish Society and St. Vincent de Paul Society, Protection for Irish Immigrant Girls Landing in Port of Boston* (Boston: 1896), pp. 3–7; Ring to Mulry, 15 April 1896, Ring Papers. For other comments on the absence of prostitution among the Irish, see William I. Cole, "Criminal Tendencies," in ed. Robert A. Woods, *The City Wilderness* (New York: 1898, reprint edition, 1970), p. 172.

12. Lord, Sexton, and Harrington, *History of the Archdiocese*, 3:364–67, 371, 372; *The Working Boy*, February 1904, January 1902, January 1884, September 1894, September 1888, February 1885; *Donahoe's Magazine* 27 (February 1892):161, 162; *Illustrated Historical Sketch Marking the Tenth Anniversary of the Founding of the Working Girls' Home in Boston* (Boston: 1899), pp. 14, 23–30, author unknown.

13. *Report of the Particular Council of Boston for the Year Ending December 31, 1889, Society of St. Vincent de Paul* (Boston: 1890), p. 7; the Society averaged more than 550 members per year during the 1890s—figure computed from the Annual Reports (1890–1900) of the Particular and Central Councils of the Saint Vincent de Paul Society; Rev. Daniel T. McColgan, *A Century of Charity: The First One Hundred Years of the Society of St. Vincent de Paul in the United States* (Milwaukee, Wis.: 1951), 2:384, 385, 400, 417–20; *Report of the Particular Council of Boston, Society of St. Vincent de Paul for the Year Ending December 31, 1886* (1887), pp. 11, 12; address dated November, 1891, Ring Papers; *Report of the Particular Council of Boston for the Year Ending September 30, 1881, Society of St. Vincent de Paul* (1881), p. 5; Thomas Dwight, "Christmas Dinners for the Poor," *The St. Vincent de Paul Quarterly* 3 (November 1898):288, 289; *Report of the Particular Council of Boston for the Fifteen Months Ending December 31, 1882, Society of St. Vincent de Paul* (1883), p. 5; *Report of the Particular Council of Boston for the Year Ending December 31, 1889*, (Boston: 1890), p. 13,

14. Ring to Thomas A. Whales, 27 July 1894, Ring Papers; Ring to Susan Emery, 18 August 1897; Francis X. Corr, " 'Fresh Air'—A Boston Doctor's Plea," *The Saint Vincent de Paul Quarterly* 13 (August 1908):282, Ring letter dated 21 June 1897; Ring to John B. Cuddihy, 4 December 1895.

15. *Report of the Particular Council of Boston, Society of St. Vincent de Paul for the Year Ending December 31, 1888* (1889), pp. 6, 7; Thomas F. Ring, "Outdoor Public Relief in Massachusetts," *Proceedings of the National Conference of Charities and Correction* (Boston: 1895), p. 63; George R. Regan, "Visiting Poor Families in Their Homes," *Proceedings of the National Conference and Celebration of the Seventy-Fifth Anniversary of the Society of St. Vincent de Paul* (New York: 1909), pp. 31, 32; *Proceedings of the National Conference of the Society of St. Vincent de Paul for 1911* (Boston: 1911), pp. 245, 246. For biographical information on Ring see John Ring's "Thomas F. Ring, The American Ozanam," undated manuscript, deposited at the Boston office of the Society of Saint Vincent de Paul. For the history of social work see Roy Lubove, *The Professional Altruist: The Emergence of Social Work as a Career, 1880–1930* (Cambridge, Mass.: 1965).

16. Handlin, *Boston's Immigrants*, pp. 161, 162; Superintendent's Journal, 21 April 1870, 25 March and 10 October 1867, 18 December 1869; Ring letter, undated, Ring to Rev. William Byrne, 9 November 1880, Ring to John Gorman, 23 February 1895, Ring letter, undated, Ring to Archbishop John Williams, 25 February 1895, Ring Papers.

17. Lord, Sexton, and Harrington, *History of the Archdiocese*, 3:499–501, 531, 352; Donna Merwick, *Boston Priests, 1848–1910, A Study of Social and Intellectual Change* (Cambridge, Mass.: 1973), pp. 7, 8, 160, 161; John F. Stack, Jr., *International Conflict in an American City: Boston's Irish, Italians, and Jews, 1935–1944* (Westport, Conn.: 1979), pp. 41, 42.

18. William Cardinal O'Connell, *Recollections of Seventy Years* (Boston: 1934), pp. 2–

10; Lord, Sexton, and Harrington, *History of the Archdiocese*, 3:442–98; *The Letters of His Eminence William Cardinal O'Connell, Archbishop of Boston*, (Cambridge, Mass.: 1915), 1:149; Merwick, *Boston Priests*, pp. 151, 152, 160, 161, 181, 182; Robert Aidan O'Leary, *William Henry Cardinal O'Connell: A Social and Intellectual Biography* (Ann Arbor, Mich.: University Microfilms International, 1980), pp. 42–68, 79.

19. O'Connell, *Recollections of Seventy Years*, pp. 270, 294–99; *Boston Pilot*, 3 October 1908; Lord, Sexton, and Harrington, *History of the Archdiocese*, 3:531–35, 575–77; O'Leary, *William Henry Cardinal O'Connell*, pp. 107–13, 124, 125.

20. O'Connell to Reverend Peter Ronan, 18 September 1909; O'Connell to W. H. Hardy, 21 and 22 September 1909, Saint Mary's Infant Asylum records, Archdiocese of Boston Archives, Brighton, Mass. (hereafter cited as A.B.A.); correspondence between O'Connell and Patrick F. McDonald, 8 and 11 October 1909, Saint Mary's Infant Asylum, A.B.A.; correspondence between O'Connell and Rev. James J. Sullivan, 7 and 9 December 1908, Carney Hospital records, A.B.A.

21. Lord, Sexton, and Harrington, *History of the Archdiocese*, 3:531, 532; correspondence of religious brothers, one letter dated 23 August 1907 and another undated, correspondence of Rev. William McDonough, undated, correspondence of O'Connell, 29 July 1909, records of the Working Boys' Home, A.B.A.

22. Robert D. Cross, *The Emergence of Liberal Catholicism in America* (Cambridge, Mass.: 1958), pp. 196, 205; *Boston Pilot*, 13 August 1910; Lord, Sexton, and Harrington, *History of the Archdiocese*, 3:386, 569, 570; *Sermons and Addresses of His Eminence William Cardinal O'Connell, Archbishop of Boston*, 11 vols. (Boston: 1915–38), 7:14–33; Merwick, *Boston Priests*, pp. 169, 182, 195; William V. Shannon, *The American Irish* (New York: rev. ed., 1966), pp. 193, 194; O'Leary, *William Henry Cardinal O'Connell*, pp. 101, 165, 166, 221–24.

23. Henry F. May, *Protestant Churches and Industrial America* (New York: paperback edition, 1967), pp. 184–88, 194–96, 231; Cross, *Liberal Catholicism*, pp. 108–19.

24. John E. Sexton and Arthur J. Riley, *History of Saint John's Seminary, Brighton* (Boston: 1945), pp. 141–43; Lord, Sexton, and Harrington, *History of the Archdiocese*, 3:528–31; O'Leary, *William Henry Cardinal O'Connell*, pp. 124, 125, 131–36; "Agreement Reached by R.C. Abp. of Boston & Sup. Gen. of Sulpicians," dated 29 September 1910, records of Saint John's Seminary, A.B.A.; James Gaffey, "The Changing of the Guard: The Rise of Cardinal O'Connell of Boston," *Catholic Historical Review* 59 (July 1973), p. 240; Merwick, *Boston Priests*, p. 192; Aaron I. Abell, *American Catholicism and Social Action: A Search for Social Justice 1865–1950* (Garden City, N.Y.: 1960), pp. 88, 89, 184–86.

25. O'Connell, *Recollections of Seventy Years*, p. 311; *The Official Catholic Directory for the Year of Our Lord 1917* (New York: 1917), pp. 44, 45; *Fifth Annual Report of the Metropolitan Central Council of Boston for the Year Ending September 30, 1917* (Boston: 1918), p. 5, deposited at the Society of St. Vincent de Paul. This author counted only those institutions located within Boston proper and excluded those catering to specific ethnic groups like the Germans. Also, this estimate does not include outpatients treated by Catholic hospitals. Morris J. Vogel, *The Invention of the Modern Hospital: Boston 1870–1930* (Chicago: 1980), pp. 126–31; *Sixteenth Annual Report of the Associated Charities of Boston, November, 1895* (Boston: 1895), p. 42.

2
Bridget and Other Irish Women

> We think the rich, tender, motherly nature of the
> Irish girl an element a thousand times more hopeful
> in our population than the faded, washed-out indif-
> ferentism of fashionable women, who have danced
> and flirted away all their womanly attributes, till
> there is neither warmth nor richness nor maternal
> fulness left in them.
>
> *Harriet Beecher Stowe,*
> *"Our Kathleens and Bridgets," 1879*

The role of women in Ireland before the Great Hunger was as
predictable as the seasons. As girls, they learned to cook and
sew, keep house, and milk cows. In discovering romance they
were left to their own devices. When it came time for marriage, girls from poor families were permitted to select their
own husbands; among the more prosperous, especially when
there was a significant amount of property involved, parents
made the choice. Irish women, in addition to watching over
livestock and preparing dairy products for market, often sup-
plemented their families' income by working at home as spin-
ners. With the onslaught of the famine and the collapse of the
textile industry, their world disintegrated, and they were
compelled to seek a new life in the alien surroundings of Boston.[1]

   Because so many of them had immigrated while still single,
and because they could speak English, Irish women, unlike
later female immigrants, turned to domestic service. In Boston

in 1850, more than 2,000 Irish females worked in this occupation, generally considered menial and beneath the dignity of
native American girls. A fixture in Boston homes throughout
the second half of the nineteenth century, the Irish maid,
popularly known as "Bridget," had to overcome strong prejudice before she finally was accepted. During the 1840s and
1850s, newspaper advertisements invited only "Americans" or
"Protestant foreigners" to apply for positions as domestics. In
a six-part series in 1852, the *Boston Transcript*, a Yankee Protestant newspaper, condemned Irish servants for their careless-
ness, slothfulness, "obtuseness," "gossiping propensities,"
and ingratitude. The paper charged that they used for recreation the time allotted them by their mistresses to attend Sunday church services. A columnist in the *Pilot*, writing under
the name "Bridget," defended Irish domestics, commending
them for their diligence and conscientiousness and maintaining that some heads of household tried to discourage them
from attending Sunday Mass and engaged in ethnic slurs by
referring to potatoes as "murphies."[2]

Guidebooks advised applicants for domestic positions to
dress neatly and plainly and to make all inquiries at the side
door rather than at the front. Maids were usually required to
live in—as one homeowner said, this arrangement decreased
their chances of bringing "disease or moral contamination into
the house." The ideal servant girl was expected to be "consci-
entious, truthful, sincere, faithful and obliging." She was to
rise at dawn, comb her hair, and above all, thoroughly wash
her hands. She was not to display dissatisfaction with her
meager wages or to complain about the unsatisfactory cleaning
methods of the domestic that may have preceded her. Remember, she was told, a "new broom sweeps clean." Her approach
to housekeeping was to be systematic and thorough; no cob-
webs or dirty finger stains should appear on door panels. To-
ward her employers she was to show courtesy and deference,
resisting at all times the personal temptation to conduct a
"petty" war with the mistress of the house. And under no
circumstances was an Irish maid to expose any Protestant
children under her care to the "heretical" teachings of her
Catholic priest.[3]

According to surveys, a domestic servant in Boston at the turn of the century worked an average of eighty-five hours per week and earned a weekly salary of $4.15, including free room and board. Irregular hours were one of the worst features of domestic service. In the factories, quitting time was clearly defined by the sound of the whistle, but Irish maids were required to be on "call." After a regular workday, which usually started at six in the morning and ended at seven at night, they were required to answer the doorbell or to serve snacks to company, especially during the opera and theater seasons. This exhausting schedule was bound to take its toll on women whose health was already weakened by sicknesses contracted in Boston tenement slums. The Saint Joseph's Catholic Home for Sick and Destitute Servant Girls, established in 1866, cared for hundreds of maids, cooks, and chambermaids suffering from consumption and overwork; other women in "shattered health" found temporary refuge at the House of the Good Shepherd.[4]

During the 1880s the Women's Educational and Industrial Union recorded hundreds of protests registered by domestics against their employers, who on numerous occasions tried to cheat them of their wages. Often pay was docked for breaking dishes or, as in one case, for spoiling a dish of prunes. Wendell Phillips, the great champion of the Negro slave, once refused to pay his maid after she had left his residence without permission. Domestics were constantly berated for their "raids on the larder" and housekeeping items. Newspaper editorials in 1852 charged Irish maids with stealing sugar, tea, pies, and even coal from their employers to help needy relatives. Some did pilfer; many were accused unjustly. In 1871, an Irish domestic sentenced to jail for stealing a pencil from a boardinghouse resident was subject to intensive questioning by a police officer who wanted to know if her priest had put her up to stealing from Yankee Protestants. With the assistance of attorney Charles Francis Donnelly, the girl was proved innocent and released. On another occasion a police officer was summoned to a Boston home to inspect "a large, suspicious-looking trunk" belonging to an Irish domestic. Her employers believed the number of apples they had purchased for pie making should have produced more pies, and the maid was accused of pilfering. Taking the policeman and her accusers up to her room, she threw open the trunk, in which no apples were to be found. Her good name slighted, she quit a few days later and went to work elsewhere.[5]

Being a domestic did have certain advantages. With free room and board included in their salary, servant girls generally enjoyed a higher standard of living than did those in factories and department stores. Although a certain "social stigma" was attached to their occupation, Irish maids at least avoided the sweatshop and the tenement slum. They tended to find their employers' homes pleasant, and despite the inconvenience of being on call, the pace was less hectic than that of the factory. In most instances, they had time to read a newspaper or enjoy a cup of tea after completing their duties. Depending on their length of service and their employers, they were given Thursday and Sunday afternoons off, which allowed them to shop, visit friends, attend church bazaars, or enjoy a ride on the electric streetcar, a mode of transportation which, expanding rapidly after the Civil War into the bucolic suburbs of Brookline, Jamaica Plain, and Dorchester, increased the number of fine homes in which to work. If they worked for very wealthy families, Irish maids escaped the city's summer heat by accompanying their employers to seaside resorts on Cape Cod, in the White Mountains, or in Maine.[6]

Many employers were genuinely fond of their domestics and protected them, trying to make them feel like part of the family by listening to their personal problems and showing them how to shop for clothes and save money. As the head of one household said, "I want the love as well as the respect of my help." And if the girls wished to entertain their "young blades," they were allowed to do so, provided it was in the kitchen or on the back piazza. The maids employed by Beacon Hill resident Susan B. Cabot were even so fortunate as to be remembered in her will. Bridget T. Madden enjoyed a fine relationship with her employer, Charles Crump, a prominent Boston diamond dealer. Born in Ireland in the 1880s, Bridget

Fig. 5. Irish maid, Annie Regan.

first worked as a chambermaid in England, where in 1901 she observed the funeral procession of Queen Victoria as it wound through London. She was devoted to the Crump family. Mr. Crump was a short, stocky, full-bearded man who, according to Bridget, believed in God only when he heard thunder strike during a rainstorm. With fatherly affection, he showed Bridget how to deposit money in a savings account and during the holidays invited her to his downtown office to view a parade. She could come and go as she pleased and was allowed to have her accordion-playing companions over for entertainment. Bridget found it difficult to leave her adopted home at the time of her marriage. "I had it so good," she said. As a wedding gift Mr. Crump offered her all the furniture in her room and presented her with a gold locket. The Crumps continued to check up on Bridget long after she had left their employ.[7]

Ignoring warnings that their morals would be jeopardized by lecherous supervisors, Irish girls accepted positions as salesgirls and factory workers and by the 1880s were a major part of the estimated 20,000 females engaged in nondomestic occupations. Factory work was tedious and harsh for Boston women. The average annual salary was $269.00, or roughly $6.23 per week, based on approximately forty-three weeks, depending on fluctuations in the economy. By the time a factory worker deducted her expenses for room and board, clothing, and carfare, she had fifteen cents a week for pocket money. In department stores, salesgirls usually worked from 8:00 A.M. to 6:00 P.M., with a half hour off for lunch. They were required to stand all day, to lift heavy packages, and to speak only to customers. In the factory, women complained of being "packed like sardines in a box," of poor ventilation, and of sharing washrooms, toilets, and drinking cups with men. To reach their workbenches they sometimes had to climb four to seven flights of stairs. If they were tardy, their pay often was docked.[8]

Each trade had its own peculiar health hazards. A common sight on the streets of Boston was the seamstress wearing dark blue glasses as a result of eyestrain. Girls in the fish and food packaging industries were exposed to caustic chemicals that caused hand blisters and lung damage, particularly in those suffering from bronchitis or asthma. Women who took home piecework after closing time not only ate cold dinners but complained of fatigue and rheumatism. Employment in tobacco factories caused numerous women to prefer chewing tobacco to smoking cigarettes. Particularly dangerous was the button-making trade, where women's fingers were punctured by plunging needles. (Company officials provided untrained medical personnel to dress, free of charge, the first three injuries. After that, the employee was required to pay.) The "hacking cough" distinguished girls who worked in the straw-goods industry.[9]

The chief aim of most Irish women was to find a husband and raise a family. In 1850 the *Pilot* cautioned them to avoid marrying anyone unwilling to become a naturalized citizen, and the popular manual, *Advice to Irish Girls in America*, recommended that they refrain from marrying any suitor who drank heavily unless he promised to take the pledge at least one year beforehand. The ideal husband, wrote Father Bernard O'Reilly in his widely read book, *The Mirror of True Womanhood and True Men As We Need Them*, should possess the virtues of "goodness, purity of life, honor, truthfulness, temperance, and fortitude." Never, advised another writer for the Boston Irish monthly, *Donahoe's Magazine*, should a girl wed out of desperation or for social status. "It is a thousand times better," he said, "to pass through life solitary and companionless, than to be a discontented partner in a union unblest by love, and not lightened by God's grace." Another warned that "a sound title to position can only be got by merit; never by matrimony." Irish girls were encouraged to marry their own kind—between 1875 and 1879, the Boston Irish community averaged only fifty mixed marriages annually.[10]

An Irish wife's primary goal was to "minister to the happiness of her husband," preparing his meals and darning his socks and comforting him in "moments of professional weariness." She was to listen to him patiently, refraining from contradicting him. Under no circumstances was she to undermine his exalted position as breadwinner by going out to work. If he spent too much time at the neighborhood saloon, even after having taken the pledge, it was probably because of her poor cooking or dreary household arrangements. Priests and physicians provided Boston Irish married couples with advice on proper sexual behavior. The purpose of sex, wrote Father Thomas Gerrard in *Marriage and Parenthood: The Catholic Ideal*, was to perpetuate the human race, express affection, and calm men's lust or "concupiscence." Sexual intercourse, he said, was to be completed as quickly as possible; "to let it have its full fling" was "to lessen its keenness, destroy its power, and to render it disgusting." Abstinence from sex during Advent and Lent was sometimes recommended as a form of penance. "Common decency," in Father Gerrard's words, dictated that sexual restraint be practiced during menstruation and the time immediately following childbirth. And those who liked to drink were told not to mix liquor with sex. A woman was forbidden to douche in an effort to prevent conception, and the practice of "coitus interruptus," wrote one Catholic obstetrician, not only was sinful but could lead to "serious mental upsets."[11]

Without contraception, childbearing was seen by most Irish women as part of God's plan. The rate of infant and child mortality among the Irish, however, was almost "suicidal." In the year 1875 alone, Boston health officials reported the deaths of 4,167 children under five years of age. Of these, 2,386 belonged to foreign parents, most of them Irish. Because of defective toilets, hallways and bedrooms reeked of urine and excrement, noted one doctor in 1875, and the tenement flat during the summer months was a breeding ground for diphtheria. Other deaths could be traced to "arsenical" wallpaper. Improper nutrition compounded these problems: some Irish women fed their newborns half-baked beans, cucumbers, and even beer and gin. Irish mothers generally breastfed their young. (Some nursed their offspring for as long as two and a half years in the belief that extended breastfeeding prevented unwanted pregnancies.) Clean, pure milk was a rare commodity in post–Civil War Boston—dealers were notorious for watering down their milk, and grocers in the poorest sections of the city mixed fresh milk with that already on hand and sold it from large, open, unwashed barrels.[12]

Because of a strong addiction to tea, some Irish women suffered from nervous and digestive disorders. In trying to solve their own health problems and those of their families, they were vulnerable to charlatans peddling patent medicines and drugs. "Worm syrup," advertised in the *Pilot* in 1854, promised quick relief for "poor, puny, suffering mortals" troubled by tapeworms, and a generous application of Russian salve ointment soothed those afflicted with piles, shingles, ingrown nails, mosquito bites, ulcers, burns, and cancer. Women inconvenienced by "female complaints" or irregular menstruation were advised to purchase "Peruvian syrup" or Lydia Pinkham's popular Vegetable Compound. Often viewing physicians as "ignorant, unskillful quacks"—as some were—and suspecting them of being "overfond of sterilizing women," many females avoided medical treatment. Some, who did seek medical attention, revealed peculiar methods of self-treatment: one Irish woman, concerned about irregularities in her menstrual cycle, drank "freely of gin" in an effort to increase her menstrual flow.[13]

With their husbands away at work, Irish women assumed greater control over the family budget and the upbringing of children. They were responsible for instilling in their children the virtues of self-discipline, obedience, and respect for older people. A mother was not supposed to punish her children while she was angry. Some daughters complained that their mothers favored their sons, but parents were counseled to treat both impartially. They were encouraged to decorate their homes with pictures of the Sacred Heart, the Blessed Mother, and "a true picture of the Holy Face." No Irish home was complete without a crucifix, "the Alphabet of Spiritual Knowledge." To cultivate a wholesome imagination, mothers were cautioned to protect their children from the "literary poisons" found in the dime novel and "Seaside" romance stories. Exposing of teenagers to "sensuous music" or the "carnal pleasure" of the waltz and the polka also was discouraged: "You cannot lessen a sin by setting it to music," one Irish magazine editorialized.[14]

Irish mothers rarely discussed sex with their children, afraid that it would be tantamount to dropping "lighted matches in a powder factory." Careful guidelines, however, were set forth in Catholic childrearing manuals. Masturbation could cause nervousness or lead to a loss of memory; if a mother discovered her children practicing that "solitary sin," she was to make every effort to prevent them from doing it again. Nocturnal emission, or "the relief of nature in the night," was considered normal as long as it did not result from youngsters' "tampering" with themselves. The generally accepted answer to a child's inquiry about where babies came from was found in the "time-honored stories of the stork and the doctor." Only if the children persisted in their questioning were they told the facts of life. Omitted from the lesson was any "full and particular description of the sexual act." When a daughter exhibited "the first signs of womanhood," a mother was advised to take the girl aside and, using the life of the Virgin Mary as a model, speak to her on the virtues of purity. Mothers were to discourage their daughters from inserting any foreign substance into the vagina for purposes of hygiene. This practice, Catholic physicians noted, not only destroyed the physical evidence of virginity but could also serve as a "stimulus to masturbation."[15]

Survival was more important than sex education to Irish women whose husbands had deserted or were deceased. (An estimated 22 percent of Irish households in 1870 were headed by women, who kept their families together by obtaining employment, sometimes aided by private charities or regular allowances from relatives back home.) In old age, Irish widows sometimes had no alternative but to seek admission to public institutions or to the Catholic Home for Aged Poor. Particularly vulnerable during hard times were large numbers of unmarried Irish females. In 1881 a lonely, crippled woman's fare back to Ireland was paid by a non-Catholic charitable agency so that she could spend her remaining days among friends and relatives. Others were not so lucky. Unemployed and impoverished, and without relatives to turn to, many simply ended up in the public almshouse.[16]

If most Irishmen believed that women should spend their energies mastering the "mysteries of the kitchen, the dining room, and the parlor," Mary Kenney O'Sullivan, Boston's most respected female labor leader, felt otherwise. Born in Mark Twain's hometown of Hannibal, Missouri, in 1864, she went to Chicago in 1878 to seek employment in order to support her invalid, widowed mother and was appalled by the factory conditions she saw there. Convinced that management was an "inhuman octopus," she organized women workers in the shirtmaking and bindery industries and became one of the founders of the National Women's Trade Union League. She refused to be intimidated or bought off by employers. During a strike, when one of the owners offered a token settlement, she declared that the workers were "out for justice, not charity." Her labor activities eventually brought her into contact with Jane Addams's Hull House, an early settlement house where she met Samuel Gompers, president of the American Federation of Labor. They took an immediate liking to each other. In the company of men, one of Mary's favorite practices was to check the inside of their derbies for a union label. On one occasion she discovered a bogus union marking in Mr. Gompers's hat. The president was properly embarrassed.[17]

In 1894 Gompers asked Mary Kenney to head an A.F.L. campaign to organize women workers in Massachusetts. While inspecting factories throughout the state, she witnessed miserable working conditions and encountered stiff opposition from management. Some factory foremen tried to discourage her organizing efforts by pointing out that their workers were mostly Catholics and consequently had to be "kept in place." At Fall River, addressing an assembly of female textile workers, she noticed that their teeth frequently were broken or missing and discovered that this was caused by their being required to break the threads by biting them. During her travels she met and married John F. O'Sullivan, a labor reporter for the *Boston Globe*. Their home in the South End soon became, in Mrs. O'Sullivan's words, "like the cradle of a newborn movement." There the O'Sullivans discussed labor problems with such guests as Louis D. Brandeis, a former corporation lawyer, and Andrew Furuseth of the International Seamen's Union. Enlightening the neophyte social reformer, Mr. Brandeis, was a challenge. "He had been thinking on the other side so long," Mrs. O'Sullivan recalled. She effectively organized women in the rubber, baking, and sheepskin industries and was responsible for legislation requiring pure milk and safety regulations to prevent laundry workers from having their arms and fingers mangled by washing machines.[18]

A member of the Massachusetts Woman Suffrage Association, Margaret Lillian Foley became one of the most articulate and colorful champions of women's rights in the United

States. Like Mary O'Sullivan, her roots were working-class. Born in the Meeting House Hill district of Dorchester in the 1870s, she attended public schools and upon graduation went to work in a hatmaker's factory. Following a brief stay with relatives in California, where she earned her keep by giving swimming and gymnastics lessons, she returned to her old job in Boston and became involved in the trade union movement of the early 1900s. A highly effective public speaker, she addressed hundreds of public gatherings, maintaining that, if given the vote, women could become a strong moral force for better factory conditions and honest government. As a consequence of her oral jousts with anti-suffragette politicians, Foley earned the titles of the "Grand Heckler" and the "Arch Quizzer." Campaigning for women's rights against Louis A. Frothingham, the unsuccessful Republican candidate for governor in 1911, she pursued him throughout the Berkshires in an automobile known as the "big suffragette machine," wearing a yellow banner demanding "women's rights now." Wherever Frothingham spoke, she interrogated him on his anti-suffrage stance. Frustrated, the candidate ordered his campaign band to strike up a tune as soon as she opened her mouth. Her supporters on one occasion attacked the musicians, causing one drummer to take refuge behind his instrument.[19]

"Maggie," as Foley's critics liked to call her, sometimes went as far as Nevada in behalf of women's rights. In 1914 the Silver State placed before its male voters a referendum on the women's question, and she crisscrossed the state for two months, talking to more than 20,000 men. She braved dust storms, rode horseback, and socialized with ranchers and cowboys who often proposed to her. On one occasion she donned the trousers and coat of a miner, and in Virginia City she descended 2,500 feet underground to persuade "husky, red-blooded men" to join her cause. Nevada women obtained the right to vote in 1914; in Massachusetts they received it six years later. With the passage of the Nineteenth Amendment in 1920, one of Miss Foley's lifelong objectives was finally achieved.[20]

NOTES

1. Joseph J. Lee, "Women and the Church Since the Famine," in *Women in Irish Society: The Historical Dimension*, ed. Margaret MacCurtain and Donncha Ó Corráin (Dublin: 1978), pp. 37, 38; T. P. O'Neill, "Rural Life," in *Social Life in Ireland, 1800–45*, ed. R. B. McDowell (Dublin: 1957), pp. 43–56; Lynn Hollen Lees, *Exiles of Erin: Irish Migrants in Victorian London* (Ithaca, N.Y.: 1979), pp. 31, 32, 106–8, 142–47; Emmet Larkin, "The Devotional Revolution in Ireland, 1850–75," *American Historical Review* 77 (June 1972):626, 627. For somewhat contradictory but important material on Irish family life see Conrad M. Arensberg and Solon T. Kimball, *Family and Community in Ireland* (Cambridge, Mass.: second edition, 1968) and Alexander J. Humphreys, *New Dubliners: Urbanization and the Irish Family* (London: 1966).

2. David M. Katzman, *Seven Days a Week: Women and Domestic Service in Industrializing America* (New York: 1978), pp. 66–69; Stephen Steinberg, *The Ethnic Myth: Race, Ethnicity, and Class in America* (New York: 1981), p. 160; Carl N. Degler, *At Odds: Women and the Family in America from the Revolution to the Present* (New York: paperback edition, 1981), p. 139; Oscar Handlin, *Boston's Immigrants, A Study in Acculturation*, rev. and enl. ed. (Cambridge, Mass.: 1959), pp. 61, 62; Mary Gove Smith, "Immigration as a Source of Supply for Domestic Workers," reprint from the *Federal Bulletin* 3 (April 1906):1–6; *Boston Transcript*, quoted in *Boston Pilot*, 2 January 1847; *Boston Transcript*, 8 March 1850, 2, 4, 5, 7, 9, and 11 February 1852; *Boston Pilot*, 14, 21, 28 February, 6 and 13 March 1852.

3. *Plain Talk and Friendly Advice to Domestics with Counsel on Home Matters* (Boston: 1855), pp. 15, 17–20, 27, 32, 65–67, 155, author unknown; "Trained and Supplemental Employees for Domestic Service," in Massachusetts Bureau of Statistics of Labor, *Thirty-Seventh Annual Report* (Boston: 1907), p. 107.

4. "Hours of Labor in Domestic Service," *Massachusetts Labor Bulletin*, no. 8 (October 1898), pp. 13, 22–26; Women's Educational and Industrial Union, "Conditions in Domestic Service—Wages," *Bulletin of the Domestic Reform League* 3 (January 1909), pages unnumbered; Massachusetts Bureau of Statistics of Labor, *Third Annual Report* (Boston: 1872), p. 64; *Fifth Annual Report of the Board of Health of the City of Boston, for the Year Ending April 30, 1877*, p. 32; Robert H. Lord, John E. Sexton, and Edward T. Harrington, *History of the Archdiocese of Boston*, 3 vols. (New York: 1944), 3:371; *First Annual Report of the St. Joseph's Home for Sick and Destitute Servant Girls* (Boston: 1869), pp. 12–15, author unknown, Boston Public Library; *Boston Republic*, 17 June 1886.

5. The logbook of the Secretary of the Women's Educational and Industrial Union, 1878 to 1894, is deposited at the Union's headquarters on Boylston Street, Boston, Mass.; Massachusetts Bureau of Statistics of Labor, *Thirty-Seventh Annual Report*, p. 106; *Boston Transcript*, 5 February 1852; Journal of the Superintendent of the Home for Destitute Catholic Children, 19 October, 15 December 1871; Edward H. Savage, *Police Records and Recollections: Or, Boston by Daylight and Gaslight for Two Hundred and Forty Years* (Boston: 1873), pp. 274–76.

6. "Conditions in Domestic Service—Wages," *Bulletin of the Domestic Reform League* 3 (January 1909), ibid. 2 (December 1907), ibid. 3 (March 1907), pages unnumbered;

"Hours of Labor in Domestic Service," *Massachusetts Labor Bulletin*, no. 8 (October 1898), pp. 27, 28; Mary W. Dewson, "Social Conditions in Domestic Service," *Massachusetts Labor Bulletin*, no. 13 (February 1900), 7–14.

7. Massachusetts Bureau of Statistics of Labor, *Thirty-Seventh Annual Report*, pp. 96–99, 105; "Social Conditions in Domestic Service," *Massachusetts Labor Bulletin*, no. 13 (February 1900), pp. 11, 12; *Boston Sunday Herald*, 27 January 1907; *Boston Post*, 30 March 1907; author's interview in 1976 with Bridget T. Madden Burns.

8. *Donahoe's Magazine* 14 (November 1885):408–10; ibid. 36 (July 1896):84, 85; Carroll D. Wright, "The Working Girls of Boston," in Massachusetts Bureau of Statistics of Labor, *Fifteenth Annual Report* (Boston: 1884), pp. 3, 34, 35, 52–54, 57, 66–71, 109, 110, 119, 127, 128.

9. Wright, "The Working Girls of Boston," pp. 71–75.

10. *Boston Pilot*, 11 May 1850; Sister Mary Frances Clare, *Advice to Irish Girls in America* (Boston: 1881), pp. 146, 147; Bernard O'Reilly, *The Mirror of True Womanhood and True Men As We Need Them* (New York: 1881), two volumes in one, vol. 1, p. 262; *Donahoe's Magazine* 21 (January 1889):46; ibid. 20 (October 1888):326; these figures were computed from marriage records at the Archdiocese of Boston Archives, Brighton, Mass. (hereafter cited as A.B.A.). For additional information on intermarriage among the Irish see Frederick A. Bushee, *Ethnic Factors in the Population of Boston* (New York: 1903, reprint edition, 1970), pp. 135–48.

11. O'Reilly, *The Mirror of True Womanhood*, part 1, pp. 57–65; Clare, *Advice to Irish Girls*, pp. 146, 147; *Donahoe's Magazine* 13 (May 1885):437, 438, ibid. 29 (May 1893):631; Rev. Thomas I. Gasson, S.J., "The Cry of the Children," ibid. 47 (February 1902):137; Lee, "Women and the Church," pp. 39, 40; Reverend Thomas J. Gerrard, *Marriage and Parenthood: The Catholic Ideal* (New York: 1911), pp. 84, 85, 88–90, 96, 98; *Sacred Heart Review*, 29 November 1890; Frederick L. Good, M.D. and Reverend Otis F. Kelly, M.D., *Marriage, Morals and Medical Ethics* (New York: 1951), pp. 141, 144. Dr. Good began practicing in Boston in 1916. Although published in 1951, this work represents the traditional Catholic physician's approach to sexual behavior in the early twentieth century. This author was unable to find statistics pertaining to the number of Boston Irish women who may have had abortions. Dr. P. O'Connell noted in 1887 that abortion in Chicago was "becoming common among Irish females—I cannot call them women. This detestable sin and most foul form of murder, shockingly prevalent among Irish Americans, is but the natural outcome of the public . . . school system of instruction without God, and the entire neglect of parental control over the children." Arthur Mitchell, "A View of the Irish in America: 1887," Éire-Ireland 4 (1969):10.

12. Bushee, *Ethnic Factors*, pp. iv, v, 44; W. L. Richardson, M.D., "Infant Mortality," in Boston Board of Health, *Fourth Annual Report* (Boston: 1876), pp. 57–70; *Eleventh Report of the State Board of Health of Massachusetts for the Six Months Ending June 30, 1879* (Boston: 1879), p. 21. Extended breastfeeding was used also by the Puritans at Plymouth (John Demos, *A Little Commonwealth: Family Life in Plymouth Colony* ([New York: 1970], p. 133); Thomas E. Cone, Jr., M.D., "Highlights of Two Centuries of American Pediatrics, 1776–1976," *American Journal of Diseases of Children* 130 (July 1976):768–70; Dorothy Therese Scanlon, "The Public Health Movement in

Boston, 1870–1910"(Ph.D. diss., Boston University, 1956), pp. 242–85. In a study of pupils attending the Boston public schools, Dr. Henry P. Bowditch, a Harvard Medical School physiologist, maintained that, because of inadequate diets, schoolchildren born of Irish parents on average weighed ten pounds less and were one inch shorter than their American classmates. H. P. Bowditch, M.D., "The Growth of Children," *Eighth Annual Report of the State Board of Health of Massachusetts, January, 1877* (Boston: 1877), pp. 275–326.

13. George Derby, M.D., "The Food of the People of Massachusetts," *Fourth Annual Report of the State Board of Health of Massachusetts* (Boston: 1873), p. 255; *Boston Pilot*, 1 July and 2 September 1854; *Boston Republic*, 1 April 1882; *Donahoe's Magazine* 40 (July 1898), page unnumbered; Sarah Stage, *Female Complaints: Lydia Pinkham and the Business of Women's Medicine* (New York: 1979), pp. 62, 63, 88, 93; *Sacred Heart Review*, 14 March 1891, deposited at St. John's Seminary Library, Brighton, Mass.; Dr. Malcolm Storer to Monsignor O'Connell, 4 June 1910, Saint Elizabeth's Hospital folder, A.B.A.; *Journal of the Gynecological Society of Boston* 5 (1871):167–69.

14. O'Reilly, *The Mirror of True Womanhood*, vol. 1, pp. v, vi, 130–44, 228, 229, 251, 279; *Sacred Heart Review*, 1 June 1889, 14 June 1890; *Donahoe's Magazine* 2 (December 1879):552. Three articles this writer found particularly helpful in approaching the study of family life and child-rearing were William E. Bridges, "Family Patterns and Social Values in America, 1825–1875," *American Quarterly* 17 (Spring 1965):3–11; ibid., Edward N. Saveth, "The Problem of American Family History," 21 (Summer 1969):311–29; and Jay E. Mechling, "Advice to Historians on Advice to Mothers," *Journal of Social History* 9 (Fall 1975):44–63; *Sacred Heart Review*, 2 February and 27 July 1889; *Donahoe's Magazine* 7 (June 1882):544; ibid. 8 (October 1882):384; ibid. 14 (November 1885):453; ibid. 20 (December 1888):552, 553.

15. *Boston Pilot*, 16 August 1913; Gerrard, *Marriage and Parenthood*, pp. 139–49; Good and Kelly, *Marriage, Morals and Medical Ethics*, p. 42.

16. Elizabeth Hafkin Pleck, *Black Migration and Poverty, Boston 1865–1900* (New York: 1979), pp. 166, 190, 191. The number of female-headed Irish families in the South End in 1880 has been estimated at 27 percent. See Stephan Thernstrom, *The Other Bostonians: Poverty and Progress in the American Metropolis 1880–1970* (Cambridge, Mass.: 1973), p. 213; *Twelfth Annual Report of the Associated Charities of Boston, November, 1891* (Boston: 1891), p. 42; James S. Sullivan, *One Hundred Years of Progress: A Graphic, Historical, and Pictorial Account of the Catholic Church of New England* (Boston: 1895), pp. 245–47; William A. Leahy, "Archdiocese of Boston," in *History of the Catholic Church in the New England States*, ed. William Byrne (Boston: 1899), 2 vols., 1:186, 187; *Boston Republic*, 29 April 1882. In 1870 and 1880, one-fourth of all Irish widows lived with their children or relatives. Pleck, *Black Migration*, p. 191; *Second Annual Report of the Associated Charities of Boston, November, 1881* (Boston: 1881), p. 26.

17. *Donahoe's Magazine* 6 (July 1881):22; Mary Kenney O'Sullivan, "Autobiography," manuscript in O'Sullivan files in Schlesinger Library, Radcliffe College, Cambridge, Mass., pp. 1, 16–34, 44–48, 62–72, 82, 83, 88, 201; newspaper clipping dated 12 February 1933, O'Sullivan file; Charles Shively, "Mary Kenney O'Sullivan," in Edward T. James, ed., *Dictionary of American Biography, Supplement Three, 1941–1945* (New York: 1973), 575, 576.

18. Allon Gal, *Brandeis of Boston* (Cambridge, Mass.: 1980), pp. 15, 57–59; O'Sullivan, "Autobiography," pp. 115–37, 143–58, 170–72, 179, 197, 230.

19. Newspaper clippings dated 30 September 1911 and 7 June 1912, Foley file, Schlesinger Library; newspaper clippings dated September and October 1911, Foley file; Michael E. Hennessy, *Four Decades of Massachusetts Politics, 1890–1935* (Norwood, Mass.: 1935), 159. For Irish Catholic attitudes on women's rights see James J. Kenneally, "Catholicism and Woman Suffrage in Massachusetts," *Catholic Historical Review* 53 (April 1967):43–57.

20. Foley file, newspaper clippings dated 10 and 11 October 1911 and 22 November and 20 December 1914.

3

The Little Green Schoolhouse

No one can get too much education.

Boston Pilot, 1915

One of the most striking anomalies of nineteenth-century Boston was the way learning and education flourished alongside poverty. Heir to a rich intellectual tradition that dated from the Massachusetts Bay Colony, Boston in the nineteenth century was a center for influential publishing houses, reform societies, and literary circles graced by the likes of Oliver Wendell Holmes, Ralph Waldo Emerson, and James Russell Lowell. The city's reputation as the "Athens of America" was enhanced by its proximity to Harvard College and a public school system described as "the richest jewel in New England's crown."[1]

Migrating from a land where nearly 50 percent of the population was unable to read or write, Irish parents found in Boston unusual opportunities for their children. With the sudden enrollment of thousands of Irish children in the public schools during the 1840s, the system underwent radical transformation. From a primary and grammar school population of about 12,000 in 1841, school enrollment had skyrocketed to more than 21,000 ten years later. Even before the Irish arrived, Boston public schools were already having difficulty meeting the educational requirements of a steadily expanding city. School officials in the 1830s complained that many of the wooden-framed schoolhouses were overcrowded, poorly ventilated, vulnerable to fire, and located in noisy, congested sections of the city where businesses, hotels, taverns, and "resorts of licentiousness" abounded. On various occasions, one school served as a makeshift fire and police station, a house of worship, and, during a cholera epidemic, a medical supply depot.[2]

In 1849, Boston police officials cited 1,066 cases of vagrancy or truancy, most of them involving children of foreign or Irish parentage. Some would hawk newspapers on busy street corners or gamble in alleyways along the waterfront; others would scurry about the rubble of recently demolished buildings, searching for firewood to heat the family's apartment or damp basement quarters. Noting that the "Police-man's badge and staff" did not frighten the truants, one official recommended either "penal legislation" or compulsory school attendance laws as a solution to the problem. To ensure that not just truants but every immigrant Irish child adopted "American feelings" and was "morally acclimated to our institutions," Horace Mann, the Secretary of the State Board of Education, and other Yankee educators successfully lobbied for the nation's first compulsory state attendance law in 1852. The statute required every child between the ages of eight and fourteen to attend school for at least three months annually. Almost immediately the *Pilot* criticized the statute for sanctioning the belief "that the education of children is NOT the work of the Church, or of the Family, but that it is the work of the State."[3]

Who, ultimately, was responsible for the child's education—church, parent, or state—was a question that provoked bitter confrontations between Boston's Irish Catholics and Protestant public school officials throughout the nineteenth century. One of the earliest clashes was the Eliot School case in 1859. Accounts varied widely, but apparently in March of that year, Irish students attending the Eliot Public School in the North End were required to recite the Protestant version of the Ten Commandments and to read from the King James Bible. Learning of this, the parish priest of a boy named Thomas Wall advised him not to comply. The boy, and some of his classmates, determined not to repeat those "damned

Yankee prayers," defied their teacher's order to read from Protestant scripture. Singled out as the ringleader, Wall was beaten with the rattan for thirty minutes by a submaster at the school and, according to some accounts, nearly fainted from loss of blood.[4]

John Bernard Fitzpatrick, the Catholic Bishop of Boston, noted privately that "much excitement" had resulted from the Eliot School incident. But with few parochial schools in existence, the Bishop could only plead with Catholic parents to be patient. In a letter to the Boston School Committee (printed in the *Pilot*), Fitzpatrick warned Protestant teachers not to use the public school classroom to undermine the Catholic faith. Meanwhile, the charges of assault and battery brought by Wall's father against the submaster in court were dismissed on the grounds that religious instruction, irrespective of anti-Catholic bias, was as much a proper function of the public school instructor as was the teaching of the three Rs.[5]

Public school readers and primers also emphasized that success would come to those who respected authority, told the truth, and avoided idleness, profanity, Sabbath breaking, tobacco smoking, and intoxicating spirits. America's egalitarian principles and disdain for caste were lavishly praised in every history and geography book. If he attended to his learning, maintained one primer, any youngster could become president of the United States. With their flag "known and respected by every civilized nation," Americans, it added, were "among the most intelligent, industrious, and enterprising people in the world." The American Indian, or Red Man, was admired for enduring pain "without uttering a groan" and for extraordinary feats such as running seventy to eighty miles in a day. He was, however, commonly depicted with tomahawk in hand, scalping women and children outside their frontier cabins. As for Negroes, the schoolbooks of the day avoided any direct condemnation of the evils of slavery. Negroes were usually shown picking cotton in the Deep South; their African ancestors were categorized as mere "savages" who engaged in tribal warfare and sold their brothers into bondage. Christian nations were "the most enlightened and powerful in the world," and Protestant countries, notably England, Germany, and Holland, won high praise for their learning, ingenuity, and industriousness; the achievements of Catholic Spain, Portugal, France, and Italy were considered less noteworthy. Inhabitants of the Iberian Peninsula were "badly governed," "ignorant and indolent," and addicted to the barbaric ritual of bullfighting. Two of the most degenerate peoples were the Russians and the Chinese. A vicious class system dominated by nobles made most Russians "ignorant, rude, and half barbarous." Also denounced for its class structure was China, where the ordinary peasant subsisted on dead cats, rats, dogs, and other "disgusting food," while the rich fared "sumptuously." Chinese worshiped false idols, distrusted foreigners, mistreated their women, and exhibited a "general disregard of truth."[6]

Primers showed a little more empathy for the plight of the Irish people under their hated master, England. "A fine, fertile" land dotted with peat bogs, Ireland, noted one primer, was exploited by landlords who lived on rents "wrung from their wretched tenantry." There were no detailed accounts, however, of the horrors endured by the Irish during the Great Famine and the mass exodus that followed. Instead there were sketches of a well-dressed Irishman and his family making their way by wagon over a village road to a seaport, where a ship and a new life as immigrants awaited them. The Irish were "generous, quick-witted, and hospitable" but were "easily offended, and prone to resentment." Exhibiting a "lively disposition," their favorite pastime was "quarrelling," using the observance of Saint Patrick's Day, in particular, as an excuse to get inebriated and break "each other's heads with clubs."[7]

Not until the 1880s, when their children made up over 50 percent of the system's enrollment, did Irish parents voice serious objection to the public school curriculum. As in the Eliot case, religion was at the center of the dispute. Prompted by complaints from some of his young parishioners attending Boston English High School, Father Theodore A. Metcalf, in 1888, accused one of the school's history instructors of making disparaging remarks about the Catholic Church's medieval practice of selling indulgences and of quoting extensively from a highly biased textbook. With Boston's twenty-four-member, publicly elected school committee almost evenly divided between Catholics and Protestants, the textbook was soon dropped, and the teacher, a zealous Congregationalist, was censured and assigned to teaching English. The controversy did not end there, however. Boston was in the grip of a national wave of nativist, anti-Catholic sentiment. This was fostered by fear on the part of a small but militant group of Protestants that certain American institutions and values—such as the public school, the free enterprise system, and political democracy itself—were being subverted by immigrant-controlled political machines, labor unions, and the nascent parochial school. Viewing the decision in the Metcalf case as an example of "Catholic intimidation," nativist Boston organizations such as the Committee of One Hundred and the Loyal Women of American Liberty attempted to purge all Catholics and their sympathizers from the school committee and other positions of public trust in the fall municipal elections. The nativist faction was led by a Baptist minister who felt ordained by God to "rid this planet of Popery" and by a woman who, claiming to be a former nun, exposed popish plots and sex orgies between priests and nuns. The election campaign of 1888 quickly degenerated into "the most disgraceful page" in the municipal history of Boston.[8]

With the defeat of Boston's first Irish Catholic mayor, Hugh O'Brien, and with only a handful of Catholics remaining on the school committee, the election clearly was a victory for anti-Catholic "fanaticism." Politically weakened, Catholics could only protest in vain two years later against another school textbook that, they felt, was riddled with "inaccuracies and fabrications" about their Church. School committeeman Joseph D. Fallon, a Catholic, who had earlier withdrawn his two daughters from the public schools because of "intolerable bigotry," resigned his seat. In 1890, after much deliberation, the *Pilot* finally implored its readers to "Multiply the Catholic schools."[9]

This was much easier said than done. In 1884 a directive issued by the American Church hierarchy had urged pastors to do everything in their power to build parish schools, but Boston had surprisingly few. From the beginning, the movement was hindered by inadequate funding, poor physical facilities, and a shortage of qualified teachers. One of the city's early parish schools, Saint Mary's, founded in 1849, was sandwiched between tenement houses and gambling establishments in the North End, where the air reeked of nearby stables and water at low tide, and where rats as big as cats raced about. Across the harbor in East Boston, a major debarkation point for Irish immigrants, a contingent of Notre Dame de Namur sisters, approximately a decade later, conducted their first classes in a ramshackle meetinghouse unprotected from chilly winds off the water. Commuting by horse and buggy from three recently opened parish schools to their convent at the parish of the Most Holy Redeemer, the Notre Dame sisters struggled to keep up with their exhausting teaching schedules, which often included collateral duties such as Sunday School instruction and First Holy Communion and Confirmation classes. They were plagued by overwork, frequent transfers, poorly ventilated and overcrowded classrooms, and cases of tuberculosis. As a result, novices with little practical teaching experience sometimes had to be pressed into service. The living accommodations of the nuns also left much to be desired. One sister wrote of the dining facilities at Holy Redeemer that "unless you were at the end of the table you might as well give up the idea of leaving before the rest of the community as you were hemmed in on all sides, like the Israelites of old."[10]

Many Irish parents believed that in the public schools their children would receive a better education and would assimilate more readily into American society. Just "because a sister or a nun wears a veil, it by no means follows that she is competent to teach," declared one Catholic in 1882. "What is in the head, and not what is on the head settles that question." To prevent Catholic defections to the public school, parish priests resorted to "entreaties and threats." In Our Lady of

Perpetual Help Parish, Father Augustine McInerney, who was the moving force behind the construction of his parish's school in 1889, chastised parents who felt they had fulfilled their obligations as Catholics simply by sending their youngsters to Sunday School classes. When persuasion did not work, a few priests denied their parishioners the sacraments.[11]

Father Thomas Scully, another strong advocate of Catholic education, blamed the slow development of parochial schools in the archdiocese on his fellow priests, who for the most part were graduates of public schools and did not share his fear of such secular institutions. Archbishop John Williams, the chief prelate of Boston between 1866 and 1907, was himself the product of a public school education and set a low priority on parish school building, deciding instead to use whatever funds he had available to erect new churches and charitable institutions. He also issued a directive ordering priests to desist from withholding the sacraments from those who disagreed with them on the School Question. Scully and other parish priests, of their own initiative, became the leaders of the parochial school movement and were known collectively as the "Schoolmen." Through the *Sacred Heart Review*, a weekly written mostly by priests, they continuously admonished those Catholic parents who considered the public schools "good enough for them," maintaining passionately that the School Question was nothing less than a "civil war." At the beginning of each school year, the *Review* reminded its readers of their solemn obligation to send their children to parochial schools.[12]

If Catholics were divided on the merits of the parochial school, nativists in Boston during the 1880s were united in their opposition to it. Encouraged by the strong showing of the state Republican party at the polls in 1887, nativist Protestants launched a full-scale legislative attack on the parochial school. With the aid of some anti-Catholic members of the Massachusetts State Board of Education, they introduced legislation that would have granted local school committees the unprecedented authority to determine whether Catholic or any other private schools should be accredited. Many educators saw a need for more systematic state supervision of curriculum, attendance regulations, and teacher qualifications, but the real intent of the inspection bill was to legislate the embryonic parochial school system out of existence.[13]

Acrimonious public hearings on the inspection bill were held in the spring of 1888. Called the "Inquisition" by the *Pilot*, they attracted numerous "cranks and wrong heads" who vilified parochial schools as alien, un-American institutions. But some of Massachusetts's most distinguished Protestant leaders joined Charles Francis Donnelly, the legal counsel for the Archdiocese, in opposing the inspection bill. President Charles Eliot of Harvard University expressed fear that every local school committee election might be turned into a political donnybrook between nativists and Catholics, or that such legislation could backfire by making Catholics even more determined to build separate schools. The most eloquent defense of Catholic and private education came from Thomas Wentworth Higginson, the grand old man of New England abolitionism and other reform causes. Describing himself as "a Protestant of the Protestants," he poignantly recalled his first lessons in religious bigotry as a child in 1834, when he witnessed a Protestant mob setting fire to the Catholic Ursuline Convent in Charlestown. He described how, during the Know-Nothing mania of the 1850s, the Irish had restrained themselves from confrontation with the Protestant nativists who paraded in torchlight procession through their neighborhoods.[14]

The most objectionable aspects of the inspection bill were defeated. To convince still-skeptical Catholic parents that parish schools were superior, publications like the *Sacred Heart Review* publicized the construction of new parish schools and gave extensive coverage to their academic accomplishments. A model institution, noted the *Review* in 1893, was the Saint Francis de Sales School atop Bunker Hill in Charlestown, not far from the original site of the Ursuline Convent. Constructed at a cost of $100,000, the four-story, red brick building contained spacious hallways and stairways and could accommodate 600 students in its sixteen "perfectly lighted, and admirably heated and ventilated" classrooms. A pamphlet

Fig. 6. Monsignor Denis O'Callaghan (1841–1913), pastor of Saint Augustine's Parish for nearly fifty years, with graduates of the parochial high school.

outlining a curriculum very similar to that in use in the public school was widely circulated throughout the parish just prior to opening day, and the *Review* noted that some of the sisters, prior to entering the convent, had taught in public schools.[15]

The magnificent Saint Augustine's Church and its "elegantly equipped" parish school in South Boston were testimony to the resoluteness of its pastor, Monsignor Denis O'Callaghan, a native of County Cork. The indefatigable fund-raiser liquidated a $250,000 debt on the church and secured an additional $100,000 for the parish school, which opened its doors in 1895. When fire razed the school in 1904, the parishioners rallied solidly behind him in rebuilding it. Throughout the entire crisis, noted a teacher, not a single student "left us for the Public School." Saint Peter's Parish, established by Irish-born Father Peter Ronan in a Dorchester meetinghouse, was "pinched with poverty" in the 1870s. An organizer blessed with "unusual common sense," Ronan managed over the succeeding three decades to build a church, a rectory, a convent, and finally, after overcoming some parish opposition, a parochial school in 1898. He was often seen climbing the scaffolding to inspect the progress of his workmen.[16]

The development of parochial schools in general was still far from satisfactory. Father Louis Walsh, the supervisor of Boston Catholic schools, noted in 1899 that some schools were hemmed in by tenement houses that cut off sunlight, a condition that impaired pupils' eyesight, he believed. Few playgrounds existed in the congested neighborhoods where many parochial schools were located, and recess in the open air was a rare treat. Overcrowding caused boys and girls to be "promiscuously placed" in the same classrooms, and, with individual classes of as many as 130, some sisters promoted children prematurely in order to accommodate incoming students.[17]

Father Walsh's duties as supervisor were frustrated periodically by pastors who viewed his personal inspections as an intrusion into their parish affairs. Textbooks were outdated and curricula varied widely, depending on which religious community was in charge of a particular school. When certain parochial schools modeled their courses after those of the public schools, these parochial schools, oddly enough, lost students because parents no longer felt that there was anything unique about them except for religious instruction.[18]

Nuns and brothers provided the inexpensive labor that helped make the parochial school economically feasible. Prior to the 1890s, however, when religious communities began to establish their own teachers' colleges, most parochial school teachers had little formal training. While Walsh encountered many capable instructors when making his rounds, he also found "a sprinkling of poor teachers." He observed that one novice, hurried into running a kindergarten class at Saint Mary's in Charlestown, was too "nervous and too impatient for such active youngsters," and a sister with more than twenty years of classroom experience, he sadly concluded, "would never be a teacher."[19]

The anemic appearance and poor health of some teachers, Walsh noted, was attributable to community regulations which required its members to rise early for exhausting prayer sessions that sometimes lasted for two hours. In addition, the intellectual development of the sisters was limited by other community regulations. A sister belonging to the Notre Dame de Namur order was not allowed to read any book without first obtaining permission from her superior, and in the evening, at recreation time, any mention of current events or other subject matter that "savours of the world" was strictly discouraged. To upgrade the caliber of instruction and to diminish the "narrowing" influence of community living, various religious orders founded their own teachers' colleges or sent their members to the first Diocesan Teachers' Institute held at Boston College, a Jesuit institution, in the summer of 1910. Adopting a generally accepted course of study, conducting annual examinations, and designating representatives of each religious community to report directly to the supervisor of schools, Boston's parochial school system had a strong administration by 1917. But the real test of the parish school would be whether or not it could successfully transmit its values to the individual student.[20]

The most striking feature of the parochial school was its religious atmosphere. Surrounded by holy pictures, statues, and crucifixes, the Catholic student had ample exposure to the "lessons of piety and morality and reverence." Although a few rambunctious youngsters had to be tied to their chairs, disciplinary problems were kept to a minimum by the respect for sisters and brothers instilled in children by their parents. Lessons on the catechism and Christian values such as charity and unselfishness appeared constantly in Catholic school primers.[21]

Catholic schools perpetuated the stereotypes of George Washington and Abraham Lincoln and introduced the salute to the flag in 1910 in order to "stimulate patriotism" and to quiet the criticism of those who still viewed the parochial school as "alien" and "foreign." Believing, correctly, that public school texts ignored "the Catholic side of American

Fig. 7. Surrounded by holy pictures, statues, and crucifixes, Irish students attending parochial schools were exposed constantly to the "lessons of piety and morality and reverence."

history," parochial school instructors familiarized their students with the contributions of members of the faith. Frequently mentioned in parochial school geography and history books were the explorations of North America by Christopher Columbus, the Jesuits, and Hernando de Soto, as were the Marquis de Lafayette, the French nobleman and hero of the American Revolution, and "fighting" John Barry, the Irish-born naval figure. The death of Catholic Archbishop John Hughes of New York was described as one of the "principal events" in American history.[22]

Public school textbooks were less than complimentary to the Irish; parochial school primers inculcated in their readers a sense of pride. Irish American youngsters learned as much about the Wicklow Mountains and the River Shannon as they did about the Great American West and the Mississippi River. Pupils at Saint Mary's in the North End declared of Ireland that "tho' we've never seen your shores/We do your name revere," while others, at Saint John's Grammar School, learned that "when Erin first rose from the dark swelling

flood,/God blessed the green island and saw it was good."
The Irish struggle against "Iron English rule" was dramatized
in stirring accounts of peasant uprisings and speeches by Irish
patriots. Familiar to almost every child was Irish martyr
Henry Grattan's vow: "I never will be satisfied so long as the
meanest cottager in Ireland has a link of the British chain
clinging to his rags. He may be naked—he shall not be in
irons." Parochial school textbooks did not allow memories of
the Great Hunger to fade. In one story, an Irish son pleaded,
"Too oft, my mother, have we felt the hand of the bereaver.
. . . Come, let us leave the dying land, and fly unto the living."
At Saint Augustine's, Irish scenery and other reminders of
Irish culture were painted on auditorium walls and curtains,
and no graduation ceremony at Charlestown's Saint Francis
de Sales was complete without Irish music, step dancing, and
the pastor's favorite song, "The Message of the Shamrock."[23]

The parochial school perpetuated its own racial and ethnic
stereotypes. Reminded regularly of Yankee prejudices against
them, parochial school students nevertheless learned to respect Protestant Americans for being sober and hardworking.
Germans, one primer noted, were "industrious, peaceable,
frugal, intelligent, and great lovers of music, in which they
excel," and the French were "gay, fond of amusement, polite," and "first in arts and sciences." Parochial school teachers
generally described Italians as "temperate," "courteous," and
"charitable," declining to mention the opposition of Italian
nationalists to the Vatican State. *The Working Boy*, a juvenile
Catholic monthly, countered the popular conception of Italians as the "sworn enemies of soap and water" and as garlic-
breathed "peddlers of bananas" by referring to Dante, Pe-
trarch, Michelangelo, and Leonardo da Vinci. Jews usually
were mentioned only in connection with Christ's death, which
was blamed on their "jealousy" of the Savior.[24]

The American Indian and the Negro were at the bottom of
the racial ladder. Apologizing only halfheartedly for the mis-
treatment of the Aztecs, Mayas, and Incas by Spanish ex-
plorers, most parochial school textbooks presented a dual image of the Indian as a "Noble Savage" and as "fierce,"

Fig. 8. An illustration from an 1877 Boston parochial school textbook shows how some Irish Catholic children came to perceive the American Indian.

"warlike," and "indolent." Praised as "swift of foot" and as a skillful hunter who could endure great physical hardship, the Indian also was prone to superstition, lacked foresight, and committed acts of savagery. He either "gorged himself," in times of plenty, or starved. One typical illustration showed a missionary tied to a burning stake. Dancing around him were Indians in animal skins, who pulled out his fingernails, ripped open his chest, tore out his heart, and stuck "a red hot iron down his throat." Negroes were distinguishable by their "very dark" skin, "wooly hair," "flat noses," and "thick lips" and were not "intelligent or enterprising." *The Working Boy* condemned the use of the term "nigger" but published stories that reinforced the shiftless "Sambo" image.[25]

Another pervasive feature of Irish Catholic education was its strong emphasis on the work ethic. Ambition, thrift, and sobriety were emphasized in juvenile stories with titles such as "Be Up and Doing," "Work On," "Learn All You Can," and "Make Your Mark." In the tradition of *Poor Richard's Almanac*, aphorisms advised Irish youngsters: "Diligence is the mother of good fortune," "Industry and happiness are inseparable," and "From the beginning to end on yourself depend." And from a poem entitled "Room at the Top," youngsters learned:

> Fancy the world a hill, lad,
> Look where the millions stop;
> You'll find the crowd at the base, lad,
> There's always room at the top.

Though the parochial school system was supported mainly by working-class parents, it accorded little attention to labor union leaders such as Terence Powderly and Samuel Gompers. As convinced as any Calvinist of the merits of rugged individualism, the parochial school teacher seldom alluded to the exploitation of labor during the Gilded Age. One text referred to leaders of the bloody Homestead Strike as "anarchists." *The Working Boy* declared that the solution to the Labor Problem was not more legislation but less consumption of liquor. While laborers "work like horses," it said, they "spend like asses."[26]

Contending that "competition and friction" bring out the best in individuals, school supervisors like Father Walsh pushed for standardized diocesan examinations as a means of promoting academic rivalry among students attending different parish schools. The ability of Catholic schools to promote a desire for success in this world was evidenced by the small number of students entering the religious life. Of an estimated 816 girls who graduated from the Fitton Grammar School in East Boston between 1870 and 1917, only 23 became nuns. At Notre Dame Academy, a middle-class girls' school, only 35 of the 462 who graduated between 1861 and 1917 entered the convent.[27]

At select schools such as Notre Dame and the Academy of the Sacred Heart, life was radically different from that at the working-class parish school. Notre Dame Academy, situated on a five-acre estate in Roxbury, was favored by both Protestant and Catholic parents who wanted a strong elementary and high school education for their daughters. The Sacred

Fig. 9. Students at the middle-class Mount Saint Joseph Academy, around 1890.

Heart Academy, on Commonwealth Avenue in the fashionable Back Bay, numbered among its alumnae the daughters of John Boyle O'Reilly, Thomas Ring, and Mayors Hugh O'Brien and Patrick A. Collins. Taught in small groups, academy students received a classical education as well as instruction in "ladylike deportment" and good manners. To help prepare them for their future roles as wives of professional men, considerable attention was paid to the art of pleasing conversation. The academies offered sophisticated courses, including piano and violin lessons, and to smooth out any rough edges still remaining, girls like Rose Fitzgerald, daughter of Boston Mayor John F. Fitzgerald and future mother of President John F. Kennedy, made the European Grand Tour.[28]

"Modern pagan fads" such as sex education were strictly forbidden in any Catholic school, declared Archbishop O'Connell in 1909. Academy girl Mary Boyle O'Reilly confessed privately that she did not know the facts of life until she was nearly thirty. In Physical Culture, the only course mentioning human anatomy, students were instructed on the circulation of the blood, bone structure, proper nutrition, good posture, and the debilitating effects of tobacco, morphine, and alcohol. Yet any inquiry as to why boys' voices happened to change during puberty was dismissed by attributing it to anything but sexual development.[29]

At a time when most youngsters left school after the eighth grade or stayed on for two more years to earn their high school diploma, Irish students who matriculated from Boston College, Holy Cross College in Worcester, or Harvard were an unusually ambitious lot. Most of Boston's first generation of Irish Catholic college students attended Boston College, founded in 1863 by Father John McElroy, a native of Ulster. Its only building, squeezed in between a graveyard and the City Hospital on Harrison Avenue, was ideally situated, as one student quipped, in case of accident. Serving also as a high school, the college, with a modest yearly tuition of thirty dollars, attracted mostly working-class students. Classes were conducted from 8:30 A.M. to 2:30 P.M., with a short lunch break. Daily Mass was compulsory, as was attendance at the college's annual spiritual retreat. The "mystic fluid" sold as coffee in the school's cafeteria and the inadequate athletic facilities irritated students, but they most resented compulsory participation in military drill, an exercise designed to improve a young man's physical stamina and give him "a more manly, graceful bearing." College officials dropped the requirement in the 1880s, frustrated by students who deliberately broke the suspender straps holding up their uniform trousers on drill day, produced notes from their doctors excusing them from any physical exertion, and complained about the high cost of uniforms.[30]

Hoping to make theirs the "greatest Catholic College in America," Boston College officials in 1907 launched a $10 million fund-raising drive. Except for the futile effort of one Jesuit to raise an additional $300,000 for a "Daniel O'Connell Memorial Building and Irish Hall of Fame," complete with a separate museumlike alcove for each of Ireland's thirty-two counties, the campaign was a success: the college purchased a new campus site in suburban Newton, atop Chestnut Hill, welcoming the first class of commuting streetcar scholars in 1913. Among its most distinguished graduates were Dr. William Aloysius Dunn, '72, "a leader in his chosen profession," and Joseph F. O'Connell, '93, a Harvard Law School graduate, United States congressman, and prominent Boston attorney. Primarily, the college served as a training ground for future priests. Of 352 graduates before 1898, 156 entered the priesthood.[31]

Some Irish parents ignored the clergy's warnings that Harvard College would jeopardize the faith of their sons. Pleased at the prospect of mingling with "men of higher social position," the few Irish Catholics at Harvard had to put up with President Eliot's criticisms of papal doctrine and teaching. Although there was a Catholic Club on campus and the college paid a Cambridge parish church for pew space for its Catholic students, Eliot's outspoken comments on the sacraments, the priesthood, and Jesuit teaching philosophy led to the abrupt termination of the pew-space arrangement at the beginning of the century. The manner in which history was presented by Harvard professors reduced the causes of the Irish famine to unenlightened English economic policy and an "excess of rainfall." Hostility between native Protestants and Irish immigrants was attributed by Professor Edward Channing to Irish "clannishness." Before he became a United States senator and had to deal with the Irish politically, Henry Cabot Lodge, as a Harvard instructor in the 1880s, pontificated on America's indebtedness to English culture and to his Puritan ancestors and was, in Henry Adams's phrase, "English to the last fibre of his thought." The early Irish, Lodge declared in 1881, were a "very undesirable addition" to the young republic—"hard-drinking, idle, quarrelsome, and disorderly" and "always at odds with the government." A cartoon in the March 1911 issue of the *Lampoon*, a Harvard student publication, showed a man stretched out on a couch, dead drunk. The caption read, "The Glorious 17th of March."[32]

Some of Harvard's Irish American graduates were among its staunchest supporters. James A. Gallivan, a Boston politician, predicted that Harvard, as "the pulse of America's highest intellectual life," would lead the way to a greater tolerance of Catholics, and Boston attorney James E. O'Connell, a student in the early 1900s, mused, "Those were the happy days." William Stanislaus Murphy, a Boston Custom House employee, willed to Harvard his estate of more than $53,000, to assist any deserving student bearing his surname.[33]

For a people who at one time measured distance by the number of rosaries that could be said, the Boston Irish, with twenty-nine parish schools, four high schools, four academies, and one college, had come a long way by 1917. Within friendly classrooms and corridors, the Irish faith and culture were transmitted from one generation to the next. But it was misleading to assert, as one Boston educator did in 1915, that the "parochial school idea" was "now firmly fixed in the Catholic mind." Only 55 percent of Boston's parishes had elementary schools, compared to approximately 80 percent in Chicago—although part of this percentage represented parish schools established by large numbers of Germans and Poles.

minorities whose size was not significant in Boston. The only other large Catholic immigrant group in Boston—the Italians—was indifferent to the idea of supporting parish schools. The fact that by 1905 at least 25 percent of the teachers in the public school system were of Irish extraction further undermined the growth of the parochial school. Irish parents no longer looked with suspicion upon the public school as an anti-Catholic institution: consequently, over three-fourths of the city's 20,000 Irish school-age children were attending public schools in 1908. Unknown numbers of Irish parents simply decided on an individual basis what was best for their children, enrolling some in public and others in parochial schools.[34]

More than anything else, the parochial school movement and Catholic higher education were inhibited by the public schools' wide reputation for progressive education and academic excellence, coupled with the imposing Brahmin intellectual tradition—a competitive situation that Catholic educators elsewhere did not have to contend with. (When Harvard president Charles Eliot criticized Jesuit teaching methods around 1900, student enrollment dropped significantly at Boston College.) Influenced by this unique historical situation, prelates like Archbishop John Williams and Cardinal O'Connell tended to support the little green schoolhouse—the parochial school—with more rhetoric than revenue.[35]

NOTES

1. Van Wyck Brooks, *The Flowering of New England, 1815–1865* (New York: 1936), pp. 89–110, 172–95; Stanley K. Schultz, *The Culture Factory: Boston Public Schools, 1789–1860* (New York: 1973), p. 108.

2. Donald H. Akenson, *The Irish Education Experiment: The National System of Education in the Nineteenth Century* (London: 1970), p. 376; Schultz, *The Culture Factory*, pp. 280–91.

3. Schultz, *The Culture Factory*, pp. 291–306; *Report of the Annual Examination of the Public Schools of the City of Boston*, city document no. 39 (Boston: 1849), pp. 31–34; *Report of the Annual Examination of the Public Schools of the City of Boston*, city document no. 31 (Boston: 1848), p. 22; *Ninth Annual Report of the [Massachusetts] Board of Educa-*

tion, Together with the Ninth Annual Report of the Secretary of the Board (Boston: 1846), p. 95; David Nasaw, *Schooled to Order: A Social History of Public Schooling in the United States*, (New York: paperback ed., 1981), pp. 75–79; quote in Schultz, *The Culture Factory*, p. 306.

4. Robert H. Lord, John E. Sexton, and Edward T. Harrington, *History of the Archdiocese of Boston*, 3 vols. (New York: 1944), 2:587–94; Schultz, *The Culture Factory*, pp. 307, 308.

5. Lord, Sexton, and Harrington, *History of the Archdiocese*, 2:595–600; Schultz, *The Culture Factory*, pp. 307, 308.

6. Report of the Committee on Books, city document no. 21 (Boston: 1847), p. 2, 5; William D. Swan, *The Primary School Reader, Part First* (Philadelphia: 1849), pp. 44, 51, 52, 64; *A Manual of Morals for Common Schools*, Stereotype edition, rev. (Boston: 1856), pp. 1, 36, 46, 49, 54, 93, 140–43, author unknown; Samuel A. Mitchell, *Mitchell's Primary Geography* (Philadelphia: rev. ed., 1849), pp. iv, 37, 38. For lists of some of the texts used in public schools see *Rules of the School Committee, and Regulations of the Public Schools of the City of Boston*, city document no. 49 (Boston: 1849), pp. 27, 28; city document no. 8 (Boston: 1855), pp. 39–41; *Annual Report of the School Committee of the City of Boston 1877* (Boston: 1878), pp. 319–21. For the best summary of values and attitudes taught in public schools see Ruth Miller Elson, *Guardians of Tradition: American Schoolbooks of the Nineteenth Century* (Lincoln, Neb.: 1964); Thomas Wentworth Higginson, *Young Folks' History of the United States* (Boston: 1883), pp. 14, 15, 20; Roswell C. Smith, *Smith's First Book in Geography* (New York: 1848), pp. 69, 88; William C. Woodbridge, *Modern School Geography* (Hartford, Conn.: sixth ed., 1848), pp. 273, 280, 288–91, 320, 331; D. M. Warren, *A New Primary Geography* (Philadelphia: 1879), pp. 25, 26; Joseph E. Worcester, *Elements of History, Ancient and Modern* (Boston: rev. ed., 1855), p. 175; *Mitchell's Primary Geography*, pp. 32, 47, 51, 96–100, 103–8, 126, 135, 162; Warren, *The Common-School Geography: An Elementary Treatise on Mathematical, Physical, and Political Geography* (Philadelphia: 1866), p. 81; *Mitchell's School Geography*, 4th rev. ed. (Philadelphia: 1853), pp. 296, 297.

7. *Mitchell's Primary Geography*, p. 102; *Mitchell's School Geography*, pp. 242, 243, 246; Richard Green Parker, *Outlines of General History* (New York: new ed., 1849), pp. 215, 216, 229; Samuel G. Goodrich, *Peter Parley's Common School History* (Philadelphia: seventh ed., 1840), pp. 280, 281, 311–14.

8. *Donahoe's Magazine* 21 (March 1889):293; James Marvin Benjamin, *The School Question in Massachusetts, 1870–1900: Its Background and Influence on Public Education* (Ann Arbor, Mich.: University Microfilms International, June 1969), pp. 80, 81, 127, 192–206; Lord, Sexton, and Harrington, *History of the Archdiocese*, 3:100, 101, 103, 107–11, 118–24, 126; *Boston Pilot*, 23 June 1888; *Boston Evening Transcript*, 9 November 1914; John Higham, *Strangers in the Land: Patterns of American Nativism, 1860–1925* (New Brunswick, N.J.: 1955), pp. 62, 63, 81, 83; Lois Bannister Merk, "Boston's Historic Public School Crisis," *New England Quarterly* 31 (June 1958):180–82; Mary Elizabeth Blake, "The Trouble in the Boston Schools," *Catholic World* 48 (January 1889):501–9.

9. Lord, Sexton, and Harrington, *History of the Archdiocese*, 3:124–26; *Donahoe's Magazine* 21 (March 1889):293, ibid., H.L.R., "Judge Fallon's Criticism of the Boston

School Committee," 25 (January 1891):15, 16; Boston School Committee, *Minority Report of the Committee on Text-Books, on Text-Books in History in the High Schools*, school document no. 13 (Boston: 1890), pp. 4–6; *Sacred Heart Review*, 21 June 1890; *Boston Pilot*, 28 and 21 June 1890.

10. James W. Sanders, *The Education of an Urban Minority: Catholics in Chicago, 1833–1965* (New York: 1977), pp. 13, 14; "Memories of Sisters Who Died in Boston," manuscript, Notre Dame de Namur Novitiate Archives, Ipswich, Mass. (hereafter cited as N.D.A.); Sister Miriam of the Infant Jesus, S.N.D., *The Finger of God: History of the Massachusetts Province of Notre Dame de Namur, 1849–1963* (Boston: n.d.) pp. 103–8; "Annals of the Holy Redeemer Convent," vol. 1 (1860–1921), 1901, N.D.A.; "Annals of the Holy Redeemer," vol. 1 (1860–1921), July–August 1888; "Annals of Notre Dame Academy, 1854–1868," 1854, p. 7, N.D.A.; "Annals of the Holy Redeemer," vol. 1 (1860–1921), September 1893.

11. A.I.R., "Some of Our Weak Points," *Donahoe's Magazine* 7 (February 1882):100; ibid., H.L.R., "The *Boston Herald* on Parochial Schools," 26 (September 1891):211; *Sacred Heart Review*, 5 January 1889, 3 September 1892; *Boston Pilot*, 12 September 1891; Sister Agnes, "Sisters of Notre Dame in Boston," 1898, N.D.A.; John F. Byrne, C.SS.R., *The Glories of Mary in Boston: A Memorial History of the Church of Our Lady of Perpetual Help (Mission Church), Roxbury, Mass., 1871–1921* (Boston: 1921), pp. 134, 135, 138, 141, 144; Robert Aidan O'Leary, *William Henry Cardinal O'Connell: A Social and Intellectual Biography* (Ann Arbor, Mich.: University Microfilms International, 1980), pp. 14, 15.

12. Lord, Sexton, and Harrington, *History of the Archdiocese*, 3:79–84, 398; Rev. Thomas Scully, "The School Question," *Donahoe's Magazine* 7 (February 1882):130; O'Leary, *William Henry Cardinal O'Connell*, pp. 12–15; Mary J. Oates, "Organized Voluntarism: The Catholic Sisters in Massachusetts, 1870–1940," *American Quarterly* 30 (Winter 1978):657. Williams went so far as to lend his name publicly to a select, private, non-Catholic school, see advertisement for the Chauncy Hall School in *The Working Boy*, February 1899; *Sacred Heart Review*, 5 January 1889, 3 September 1892.

13. Lord, Sexton, and Harrington, *History of the Archdiocese*, 3:100, 101, 111–15.

14. *Boston Pilot*, 11 February, 2 June, 24 March 1888; Lord, Sexton, and Harrington, *History of the Archdiocese*, 3:115–17; *Boston Pilot*, 31 March, 7 April 1888.

15. Lord, Sexton, and Harrington, *History of the Archdiocese*, 3:132–33; *Sacred Heart Review*, 5 October 1889, 11 February 1893.

16. "Annals of St. Augustine's Convent," 1 (1895–1902):1–15, N.D.A.; *Boston Pilot*, 28 June 1890; Sister Miriam, *The Finger of God*, pp. 219–21; "Annals of St. Augustine's Convent," 2 (1903–27):14–17, 113, 108–10; Susan L. Emery, *A Catholic Stronghold and Its Making: A History of St. Peter's Parish, Dorchester, Massachusetts* (Boston: 1910), pp. 4, 8, 9, 17, 18, 22, 30, 40, 59, 60, 65, 74.

17. "Report of the Supervisor of Schools on First Official Visit, January 1898 to January, 1899: Archdiocese of Boston Parochial Schools," pp. 1–23 (hereafter cited as Walsh Report), Archdiocesan Office of Catholic Schools, Boston, Mass. For reference to premature promotion see "Catholic School Report of St. Augustine's School for the Year 1908–1909," Archdiocesan Office of Catholic Schools (hereafter cited A.O.C.S.).

18. Walsh to Rev. R. J. Johnson, 19 May 1905, A.O.C.S.; Walsh Report, 26, 27, 49–51.

19. For information on training of religious teachers see Sister Mary of the Holy Angels, *Quiet Revolution: The Educational Experience of Blessed Julie Billiart and the Sisters of Notre Dame de Namur* (Glasgow: 1966), pp. 138–43; Walsh Report, pp. 54–74. For Walsh's opinion of individual teachers, see his notes in folders on Saint Mary's School, Charlestown, dated 13 October 1904 and Saint Columbkille's School, 25 January 1904, A.O.C.S.

20. Walsh Report, pp. 57, 73; *Rules and Constitutions of the Sisters of Notre Dame* (Brussels: 1893), pp. 34, 35, 48, N.D.A.; Sister Mary Neonilla Barrett, S.S.J., "Unification of Parochial School Education in the Archdiocese of Boston" (Master's thesis, Boston College, August 1949), pp. 12–14, 38, 39, 51.

21. *Sacred Heart Review*, 11 February 1893; "Annals of St. Augustine's Convent," 2 (1903–27):65; *Report of the Proceedings and Addresses of the 6th Annual Meeting of the Catholic Educational Association* 6 (November 1909):403–5; *Sadlier's Excelsior, Second Reader*, by a Catholic Teacher (New York: 1876), pp. 21–23; *Sadlier's Excelsior, Third Reader*, by a Catholic Teacher (New York: 1876), pp. 80–84. For an exact but incomplete list of textbooks used in Boston parochial schools at the turn of the century, see individual school reports, A.O.C.S.

22. George A. Lyons, Supervisor of Boston Catholic Schools, to Archbishop William O'Connell, 17 January 1911, Supervisor of Schools file, Archdiocese of Boston Archives, Brighton, Mass. (hereafter cited as A.B.A.); *Sadlier's Elementary History of the United States*, by a Teacher of History (New York: 1896?), preface, pp. 3–11; Thomas Bonaventure Lawler, A.M., *Essentials of American History* (Boston: 1902), pp. 26, 39, 166, 194; *Sadlier's Excelsior, Fifth Reader*, by a Catholic Teacher (New York: 1877), pp. 55–58; Frank X. Sadlier, *Sadlier's Intermediate History of the United States* (New York: 1915), pp. 127, 136; Golden Jubilee Book of The Sisters of Notre Dame, compiled by students of Saint Mary's School in the North End, 1890, pages unnumbered, N.D.A.

23. Schultz, *The Culture Factory*, p. 229; Golden Jubilee Book, Saint Mary's School, 1890, page unnumbered; Golden Jubilee Book of The Sisters of Notre Dame, compiled by students of Saint John's School, North End, 1890, page unnumbered, N.D.A.; Golden Jubilee Book of The Sisters of Notre Dame, compiled by students of Notre Dame Academy, Roxbury, 1890, pages unnumbered, N.D.A.; Catholic Columbian Exhibit Book, prepared by the students of Saint Mary's School, North End, 1893, pages unnumbered, N.D.A.; *Sadlier's Excelsior, Fifth Reader*, pp. 257–60; "Annals of St. Augustine's Convent," 2 (1903–27):27, 28. Graduation exercise programs for the classes of 1912 and 1913 are in the possession of Saint Francis de Sales School officials, Charlestown, Mass.

24. Golden Jubilee Book, Saint Mary's School, 1890, page unnumbered; *Sadliers Excelsior, Geography Number One*, by a Catholic Teacher (New York: 1875), p. 31; *Sadliers' Elementary Geography* (New York: 1883), p. 61; *The Working Boy*, September 1888; Columbian Exhibit Book, Saint Mary's, 1893, p. 48.

25. Golden Jubilee Book of The Sisters of Notre Dame, compiled by students at the Holy Trinity School, Boston, 1890, pages unnumbered, N.D.A.; Lawler, *Essen-*

tials of American History, pp. 21–49; Golden Jubilee Book, Saint Mary's School, 1890, pages unnumbered; *Sadlier's Excelsior, Fifth Reader*, pp. 125–27, illustration is inside cover page; *Elementary Geography*, p. 71; *The Working Boy*, July 1886, September 1887, July 1895; Golden Jubilee Book, Notre Dame Academy, 1890, pages unnumbered.

26. My contention regarding the Catholic stress on the work ethic has been drawn from a close reading of *The Working Boy* (1885–1900) and the several cited Golden Jubilee Books deposited at the N.D.A. For some specific Catholic textbook examples of the work ethic see *Sadlier's Excelsior, Second Reader*, pp. 44–47; *Sadlier's Excelsior, Third Reader*, pp. 40–43; *The Working Boy*, September 1885. As to how pervasive it was in the Boston Irish community as a whole, see Francis Walsh, "Lace Curtain Literature: Changing Perceptions of Irish American Success," *Journal of American Culture* 2 (Spring 1979):139–46. In a diocesan examination in 1908, students were asked to identify enterprising individualists like Morse and Field rather than either Gompers or Powderly, A.O.C.S.; Lawler, *Essentials of American History*, pp. 264, 351–56, 359; *The Working Boy*, January 1889, February 1890.

27. Walsh Report, pp. 40, 90; Fitton School file, N.D.A.; *Academy of Notre Dame, Roxbury, Massachusetts, 1854–1954* (n.p.: 1954), pp. 33–35, 44, author unknown.

28. *The American Foundations of the Sisters of Notre Dame de Namur*, by a Member of the Congregation (Philadelphia: 1928), pp. 249–54; William A. Leahy, "Archdiocese of Boston," in William Byrne, ed., *History of the Catholic Church in the New England States*, 2 vols. (Boston: 1899), 1:177–80; Louise Callan, *The Society of the Sacred Heart in North America* (London: 1937), pp. 612–14, 727; *Course of Study in the Academies and Parochial Schools of the Sisters of Notre Dame* (Cincinnati, Ohio: 1895), pp. iv, v; the book containing the list of students attending the Academy of the Sacred Heart is in the possession of officials at the Newton Country Day School of the Sacred Heart, Newton, Mass.; Rose Fitzgerald Kennedy, *Times to Remember* (Garden City, N.Y.: 1974), pp. 28–33.

29. Correspondence between O'Connell and Mary Boyle O'Reilly, 15 and 22 November 1909, A.B.A; *Course of Study in the Academies and Parochial Schools of the Sisters of Notre Dame*, pp. 35–38, 52–54; Sister Barrett, "Unification of Parochial School Education," p. 20; Joel Dorman Steele, Ph.D., *Hygienic Physiology* (New York: 1884), pp. 75, 130, 170, 171, 201–3.

30. Oscar Handlin, *Boston's Immigrants, A Study in Acculturation*, rev. and enl. ed. (Cambridge, Mass.: 1959), p. 169; David R. Dunigan, *A History of Boston College* (Milwaukee, Wis.: 1947), pp. 5, 6, 8–14, 44, 97, 98; *Boston College Stylus* 4 (April 1886):31. In the college's earliest registration book, one can find the name and address of each student's father or mother. Using these data in conjunction with city directories, which list a person's occupation, the author was able to assess the socioeconomic background of individuals attending Boston College; *Boston College Stylus* 2 (September 1883):6, ibid. (December 1883):18, ibid. (March 1884):43; Dunigan, *A History of Boston College*, pp. 110–14.

31. Dunigan, *A History of Boston College*, pp. 183–200; *Boston College Stylus* 12 (January 1898):5, 7; O'Connell family records, in author's possession; *Graduates of Boston College, Boston, Mass.* (Cambridgeport, Mass.: 1897), p. 24.

32. *Sacred Heart Review*, 3 September 1892; *Report of the Proceedings and Addresses of*

the First Annual Meeting of the Catholic Educational Association (Columbus, Ohio: 1904), p. 79; John J. Ryan, "The St. Paul's Catholic Club," *Harvard Alumni Bulletin*, vol. 17, 13 January 1915, pp. 264–65. For material covered in Professor Hart's class see lecture notes of Clarence A. Bunker, Class of '89, 1887–88, Harvard University Archives; Edward Channing, *A History of the United States*, 6 vols. (New York: 1905–25), 5: 477–80, 6:131; Edward N. Saveth, *American Historians and European Immigrants, 1875–1925* (New York: 1948), pp. 54–58, 198, 199; Joseph Smith, "American History As It Is Falsified," *The Journal of the American-Irish Historical Society* 1 (Boston: 1898):82, 86; Henry Cabot Lodge, *A Short History of the English Colonies in America* (New York: 1881), pp. 228, 261, 262; *The Harvard Lampoon* 61 (3 March 1911):15.

33. James A. Gallivan, "Catholic Sons of Harvard," *Donahoe's Magazine* 32 (November 1894):510; Secretary's Report, *Harvard Class of 1902, Fiftieth Anniversary* (Cambridge, Mass.: 1952), pp. 487, 488; Marcia Graham Synnott, *The Half-Opened Door: Discrimination and Admissions at Harvard, Yale, and Princeton, 1900–1970* (Westport, Conn.: 1979), p. 10.

34. *The Official Catholic Directory for the Year of Our Lord 1917* (New York: 1917), pp. 34–36, 43–44; Rev. Augustine F. Hickey, "A Study of the Growth and Development of Catholic Education in the Archdiocese of Boston, 1907–1923," Table X, p. 46, A.O.C.S. In arriving at these figures and percentages, the author has computed only those parishes located within Boston proper and has excluded those designated as ethnic or national parishes. There were two Italian schools, one Polish, and one German. *Boston Pilot*, 4 September 1915; Sanders, *The Education of an Urban Minority*, pp. 4, 40–71; Robert A. Woods and Albert J. Kennedy, eds., *The Zone of Emergence: Observations of the Lower Middle and Upper Working Class Communities of Boston, 1905–1914* (Cambridge, Mass.: paperback ed., August 1969), pp. 204–5; Massachusetts Bureau of Statistics of Labor, *Census of the Commonwealth of Massachusetts, 1905*, 4 vols. (Boston: 1908–1910), vol. 2, *Occupations and Defective Social and Physical Condition*, p. 134; United States Immigration Commission, *The Children of Immigrants in Schools* (Washington, D.C.: 1911), 2:181, 185; O'Connell family records, in author's possession.

35. Dunigan, *A History of Boston College*, pp. 168–79; O'Leary, *William Henry Cardinal O'Connell*, pp. 12, 13, 138–40.

4

Irishmen of Wealth and Standing

The Irish are just as good at making money as the
  Yankees.

Abner and Frank Forbes, *Our First Men*, 1846

Boston throughout the nineteenth century was an excellent
place for men with ambition and some luck. Since colonial
days its merchants and traders had looked seaward for their
profits—from the Merchants' Exchange Building on State
Street they could observe ships entering the harbor laden with
treasures of Far East trade. Success in foreign commerce
whetted the profit-making appetites of prominent Yankee
families like the Lowells, the Lawrences, and the Cabots,
who, during the 1830s and 1840s, accumulated additional fortunes through investments in Massachusetts textile factories as
well as in canals, railroads, and mining projects in the West.[1]

Irish immigrants, as canal diggers, railroad workers, and
day laborers, enjoyed few of the benefits associated with this
grand world of Yankee commerce and finance. Having settled
in such large numbers, however, the Irish had created a dynamic urban ethnic marketplace that demanded more doctors,
lawyers, priests, journalists, grocers, liquor dealers, contractors, and, of course, undertakers. The Irish who provided
their countrymen with these critical services earned for themselves the enviable reputation of being men of wealth and
standing.[2]

As early as 1846 Yankee writers were commenting on the
"money-making genius" of exceptional Irishmen such as

Andrew Carney. Born in 1794, Carney emigrated to Boston in 1816 and worked briefly as a peddler. Opening a tailor shop with a partner in 1830, aided by lucrative government uniform contracts and later by the invention of the sewing machine, Carney by mid-century became "one of the wealthiest and most respected Catholics in Boston." A major benefactor of the Church, he often acted as intermediary between Yankee businessmen and the Catholic hierarchy frustrated in trying to purchase property in Boston. Through marriage he became associated with an influential Genoese trading family, and, much to his delight, the Italians named one of their clipper ships the *Andrew Carney*.[3]

Few Irishmen achieved success in such a storybook fashion. An Irish businessman usually started out by opening up a grocery store in his tenement house or elsewhere in the neighborhood, a venture that required very little capital or overhead. Providing a convivial atmosphere in which customers could congregate and purchase spirits as well as provisions, Irish grocers, numbering around 200 in 1850, competed vigorously for the patronage of their countrymen. Opening his store early in the morning, the grocer arranged his vegetables so the hot afternoon sun would not reach them, checked the barrel for spoiled apples, and placed stand-up signs outside his store announcing the latest prices. He personally inspected the lamb, pork, and beef he purchased; nothing was as embarrassing as to have a customer complain of "tainted meat." Because most of his customers were paid by their employers only once or twice a month, the grocer also had to pay strict attention to his account books.[4]

The twin hazards of the grocery trade were extending credit to neighbors unable to pay their bills regularly and consuming one's own liquor inventory instead of selling it. Some grocers succumbed to other pressures. Dennis Collins had accumulated the substantial fortune of $40,000 in 1872 by running a grocery store and dabbling in real estate. During the depression the following year, however, his business slowed down and his credit, as one agent for R. G. Dun & Company noted, was "good for 0." By 1880 he was out of business. In

Fig. 10. The O'Keeffe Grocery Store, Dorchester, around the turn of the century. The O'Keeffes later went into partnership with two other grocers to form what eventually became the First National Food Stores chain.

1858 another grocer, Daniel Kelly, was spoken of by the policeman on the beat as a "steady orderly man." But four years later, after he had married a young woman who monopolized his time, his business was reported to be "all run down."[5]

In one decade alone—1880 to 1890—an estimated 27 percent of all Irish groceries and similar small businesses folded, a fact that cannot be attributed entirely to weaknesses in Irish character, fluctuations in the market economy, or lack of business acumen. To obtain capital and credit to expand or to stay afloat, the Boston Irish entrepreneur often had to gain approval from one of R. G. Dun's agents. Following the nationwide custom of their company, Boston agents for R. G. Dun often took it upon themselves to advise potential lenders when a credit applicant was Irish, commenting on his personal life as well as on his assets, debts, and business experience. Patrick Carney, an Irish grocer and "rummy politician," was a "disagreeable man to deal with" and the alleged father of an illegitimate child, declared one agent. The Irish blacksmith John E. Gorman, noted another agent, was "too fond of horse flesh," or betting. One grocer reportedly delinquent in paying his debts was categorized as a "tricky Irishman," and an Irish tailor was suspected of liking "his whiskey too well."[6]

In 1850, more than 900 of the 1,500 Boston establishments selling liquor were Irish-operated. Numerous legislative efforts to limit and prohibit the sale of intoxicating beverages did not prevent "a reliable, close, and shrewd businessman" like Garrett Nagle from succeeding in the liquor business. James Walsh, a wholesale liquor dealer, was able to earn $75,000 between 1860 and 1875 by satisfying the thirst of his countrymen, and James Collins, estimated to be worth close to $100,000 in 1869, took pride in flying both Irish and American flags from the rooftop of his liquor store. The barons of Boston's liquor business were James William Kenney, Michael Doherty, and Lawrence J. Logan. Arriving in Boston in 1863, Kenney worked for a time in his brother's liquor store in the North End, where he learned the intricacies of the business. Possessing a "keen and grasping" intellect, he soon invested heavily in ale and porter and by 1894 owned a brewery that produced 150,000 barrels annually and was worth over $500,000. A businessman above all, he deserted the traditional allegiance of the Irish to the Democratic party in 1884 in favor of the protectionist Republican party. Michael Doherty, a power broker in the city's Democratic party and president of a brewery that was "growing stronger all the time," was described by a Dun agent in 1862 as a "pretty shrewd man and influential among his countrymen." Accused by the agent of being prone to excessive drinking and gambling, he successfully divided his time between ward meetings and his liquor store and left an estate of $145,000. Lawrence J. Logan, "a very prudent" Irishman who always watched "his interests closely," started out in his brother's liquor store in the 1860s. Purchasing great amounts of whiskey and hoarding it until prices rose, he was, in addition to being a trustee of several local banks, worth more than $100,000 by 1880 and was the father of a priest, a judge, and a Harvard College football star.[7]

To protect their interests from prohibitionists and to lure steady customers with the promise of patronage jobs, many Irish liquor dealers, like Doherty, sought and won elective office. (By the 1870s 10 to 15 percent of the Boston Common Council—representing 3,000 proprietors at a time when 20,000 votes was considered enough to elect a mayor—had

Fig. 11. Irish immigrants learned early that Boston's streets were not paved with gold, but some, as contractors, found that fortunes could be made by digging them. Here workers in 1900 are building the East Boston Subway Tunnel.

ties to the liquor trade.) John Clancy, according to one agent "a very fair risk for his class," sat on the Common Council; the saloon of John J. Teevens gave him an automatic "following," and he, like Clancy, was elected to the Common Council. Most successful in mixing beer and politics in the 1880s was Patrick J. Kennedy, an amiable, soft-spoken saloonkeeper and state representative from East Boston, paternal grandfather of an American president.[8]

Irish immigrants learned early that the city streets were not paved with gold, but some, as contractors, found that fortunes could be made by digging them. To accommodate an urban population that had mushroomed from around 93,000 in 1840 to over 560,000 by 1900, new parks, streets, homes, sewers, streetcar lines, and gas and water works had to be built. The city's annual expenditures, which included other municipal services, soared from more than $2 million in 1850 to $26 million by 1900.[9]

A "thoroughly competent and reliable" builder, Timothy H. Connolly received innumerable city contracts to dig sewers, build railroad bridges, and erect tenement houses. Between 1876 and 1895, John McNamara and Sons erected public schools, firehouses, police stations, old soldiers' homes, breweries, parish halls, Jewish temples, and "handsome private residences" in the Back Bay. Patrick O'Riorden's start in the contracting business was fortuitous. A laborer at the Boston Navy Yard in the 1860s, he was severely injured in an accident that prompted his co-workers to take up a special collection and present him with a horse and wagon. His health restored, O'Riorden began removing earth from building sites in Boston with his modest wagon and used the proceeds to speculate in real estate, which generated additional income, allowing him to purchase more teams. He secured "a great deal of government business" and by 1900 had 3,000 men on his payroll, owned 500 horses, and was reputed to be a millionaire. Charles Logue, a native of Londonderry, was esteemed as a contractor who attended to all his orders promptly. He profited substantially by erecting buildings for the Catholic Archdiocese and Boston College and, in 1912, by constructing Fenway Park, home of the city's American League baseball representative, the Boston Red Sox.[10]

Two of Boston's pioneer contractors were Timothy Hannon and Owen Nawn. Hannon broke into the contracting business during the 1840s by obtaining a few horses and making his own excavation tools. He helped to fill in Back Bay swamps and to level Fort Hill in the 1850s, and when South Boston became a haven for well-to-do individuals wishing to escape city congestion, Hannon designed and graded many of

Fig. 12. Charles Logue (1858–1919), builder of Fenway Park, and family.

its first streets and boulevards. Nawn worked in the 1850s as a stable hand and saved enough to buy horses and enter the teaming business. An "honest, energetic, frugal man," he obtained large contracts, and, by investing in cheap tenements that he rented to his employees, he was worth close to half a million dollars by 1875. Then, in the midst of a national depression, his teams were "only partially employed on transient jobs," and work in his granite pits and quarries came to a standstill. Nawn had to mortgage everything. Things picked up for him in the 1880s, when he obtained work from streetcar companies and contracts from the city.[11]

At the turn of the century, city contracts were a major source of business for Boston's 235 Irish contractors, particularly if they had friends in the mayor's office or on the Common Council. (The Nawns' residence in Dorchester, for example, was always open to Mayor John F. Fitzgerald, a neighbor, who liked to drop in for "conversation" and peanut butter sandwiches.) Because of statutes governing the awarding of contracts, Mayor Fitzgerald, elected in 1906, was in an ideal position to reward builders who had made contributions to his campaign. According to the law, any contract over $2,000 could be dispensed without advertisement, as long as the mayor approved it in writing. "Honey Fitz" found these regulations perfectly suited to his mode of government. In one year of his term, 98 of some 162 contracts awarded by the sewer department went to individuals with names like O'Brien, Rooney, and Shaughnessy.[12]

Investigations conducted by the Boston Finance Commission in 1907 and 1908 uncovered what it called "a lamentable picture of dishonesty and greed," citing cases of collusion between politicians and contractors. According to the commission, contractor Thomas Welch had become acquainted with Fitzgerald's brother during the mayoralty campaign. Following the election, Welch went to see the superintendent of streets, expecting to obtain a lucrative contract crushing stone for the city. The superintendent balked, and a perturbed Welch proceeded to visit the mayor's brother. Quizzed by the commission as to the brother's actions, Welch innocently replied, "I don't know, but the result was I got the crusher." He also confessed to giving $1,000 to councilman Philip McGonagle in the hope of landing another "gift" contract. Welch recalled that when he made part of the payoff in the corridor of the State House, the politician first felt "delicate" about accepting the money but, after some coaxing, took it.[13]

The contractor was not the only Irishman to make money by breaking ground. Throughout the nineteenth century, undertaking was a part-time occupation for a large number of church sextons and also for graveyard superintendents, livery stable owners, sporting goods salesmen, and even politicians. By 1905, 105 of the city's 252 undertakers were first- or second-generation Irish. Often working while relatives looked over his shoulder, the undertaker prepared the body at the home of the deceased, being careful not to remove any of the sacred oils used by the priest during the last rites and checking with relatives to make sure that the hair of the deceased was parted in death as it had been in life. He notified newspapers, made funeral arrangements with the parish priest, and measured the doorway to avoid the embarrassment of not being able to fit the casket through it. He also set up the chairs, candles, and crucifixes. On the day of the funeral he inspected his drivers to see that they were properly attired in dark suits and tall hats, gave final instructions to the pallbearers, sent a carriage for the priest, and made sure that no one in the funeral party had been stranded at the cemetery and that all the tools of his profession had been removed from the home of the deceased.[14]

By engaging in politics and other social activities, the Irish undertaker was able to solicit business and dispel the notion that he was "different from others." Undertaker John Reade divided his time between gatherings of the Ancient Order of Hibernians, the Charitable Irish Society, the Land League, the Grand Army of the Republic, and the Massachusetts State Legislature, where he represented his Charlestown neighborhood in 1880. A "pleasing and dignified" individual, Patrick J. Brady, one of the city's leading undertakers, campaigned for Mayor Fitzgerald and attended the Democratic National Convention in Baltimore in 1912, and Frederic J. Crosby was a member of the Boston Athletic Association, the Knights of Columbus, the Massachusetts Catholic Order of Foresters, Roxbury's Businessmen's Association, and the United Fifty. It is a wonder they found time to bury anyone at all.[15]

Agents for R. G. Dun generally found Irish undertakers to be sound businessmen. John McCaffrey paid his bills promptly and was "careful" and "shrewd," while Frederic Crosby was "an honest, young man" who took "good care" of his business. Generally passed on from father to son, undertaking provided income that allowed some practitioners to speculate in real estate. McCaffrey was worth more than $46,000 at the time of his death in 1901. John W. Lavery, who inherited his father's undertaking business and acquired substantial property, was regarded as one of South Boston's most "solid men."[16]

In response to criticism by the clergy for encouraging the Irish "passion for splendid funerals" and for using up most of the burial insurance money, undertakers protested that their suggestions for "moderation" were often disregarded by the bereaved. John D. Fallon was one Irish undertaker who was above reproach. A sexton and funeral director for nearly forty years, he buried more than 170 people in 1907. His account books reveal a meticulous and compassionate man. He itemized the cost of the casket, hearse, candles, chairs, newspaper notices, and long-distance phone calls and, when shipping a body out of state, noted whether or not there was "an undertaker at the other end." At times he waited ten years to collect a debt of less than $200 and accepted installments as small as $1 and $2. Although certain patrons owed outstanding sums, he seldom turned down a request for his services when death visited them a second or third time.[17]

Since the 1840s, when James Egan became the first Irish-born member of Boston's Suffolk County bar, the Irish had steadily filtered into the legal profession. To be admitted to the Massachusetts bar in the nineteenth century, a candidate generally had to read law in a practicing attorney's office or graduate from a law school, presenting himself to a state supreme court judge for examination. Beginning in 1876, he was required to pass a written test of some forty questions. To attract clients, some lawyers advertised in the *Pilot*. Attorney John Tighe, secretary of the Irish Emigrant Society, announced in 1850 his willingness "to defend any of his unfortunate countrymen" in court or to lend his expertise in conveyances, "the most abstruse and complicated department of legal science." After the Civil War, other lawyers offered aid in "the collection of Bounties, Pensions, Prize Money, Arrears of Pay, applications for State Aid, and all Army, Navy, and other Government claims."[18]

Most Irish lawyers were general practitioners. Speaking with "a nice Doric brogue," Thomas Riley easily charmed and persuaded juries and was worth more than $100,000 by 1900. In 1885, Thomas J. Gargan, son of a Boston Irishman who helped slaves escape via the underground railroad, enjoyed a lucrative private practice and became the first Irish Catholic to deliver Boston's Fourth of July address. Charles Francis Donnelly, born in County Roscommon in 1836, was Boston's most esteemed Irish lawyer. As a young man he worked in a law office and attended Harvard Law School. When a group of South End residents approached his employer, Ambrose A. Ranney, about taking legal action against Catholic officials wishing to purchase property for a church in the Protestant neighborhood, Ranney instructed Donnelly to draw up the necessary legal documents. The young man, who at one time had contemplated entering the priesthood, "respectfully" refused to do so, and Ranney, admiring his grit, told the Protestants to take their business elsewhere. Donnelly, who did not marry until he was nearly sixty, did his most important work as chief counsel for Boston's Catholic Church, handling real estate transactions, drawing up charters for Catholic institutions, securing the legal right of Catholic priests to visit patients in state institutions, and representing the parochial school system.[19]

To succeed as a lawyer, Donnelly declared, one should be honest, hardworking, and well educated, with experience as a lawyer's apprentice. Another attorney declared it ethically and morally repugnant to profit from the "great national wrong," divorce. John J. Corcoran, a Superior Court judge, recommended that attorneys charge "a fee and not an extortion." And although he owed his appointment to political connections, he cautioned against the "alluring voice of the siren, politics," asserting that "the shamelessness and intrigue and the selfishness of office seeking" could compromise even the most high-minded of lawyers.[20]

For many Boston Irish lawyers, however, the lure of politics was irresistible. More than half of the prominent Irish attorneys practicing between 1865 and 1917 either held elective office or were otherwise involved in politics. Because Irish lawyers were not hired by Yankee law firms and running for office helped lawyers attract new clients, many divided their time between the legal brief and the ballot box. Joseph F. O'Connell, a young Harvard Law School graduate, began practicing in his neighborhood of Dorchester in 1896 and plunged into politics in addition to handling cases ranging from nonpayment of rent and grocery bills to dog shooting

Fig. 13. Like many Boston Irish attorneys, Congressman Henry F. Naphen (1852–1905) successfully divided his talents between public service and running a private law practice.

and "animal assault" by a father upon his daughter. O'Connell, defeated in his first run for office in 1904, was elected to the United States Congress two years later.[21]

Political involvement led to appointments as municipal judges, particularly when the lower court system expanded after the Civil War. Appointed Boston's first Irish Catholic judge in 1872, Joseph Daniel Fallon attended Holy Cross College and, after briefly teaching school, studied law with a retired judge in Salem. Opening an office in Boston, Fallon soon turned to politics and in 1864 was elected the first Irish Catholic member of the Boston School Committee. Eight years later he was appointed to the South Boston District Court and earned a reputation as a "thorough, but considerate, fearless and kindly judge." He succeeded in halting the dangerous practice of children stealing rides on streetcars and as a devoted family man was especially stern with wife beaters, fathers who failed to support their families, and storekeepers who tried to sell adulterated food and watered-down milk. At the time of his death in 1917, more than half the municipal judges were Irish.[22]

Though well represented on Boston's benches, the Irish had little success in gaining appointments to the state's higher courts. Prior to the election of David I. Walsh as Massachusetts's first Irish Catholic governor in 1914, appointments to the Superior and Supreme Judicial courts went almost entirely to Yankee patricians. Of the 65 jurists appointed to the Superior Court between 1865 and 1913, only 6 were of Irish background. And during this period only one of the 28 appointees to the Supreme Judicial Court was Irish. The small number of Catholics on the state's highest tribunals was the result of a "religious cabal," according to Joseph F. O'Connell, who had returned to the full-time practice of law in Boston in 1910 after having lost a bid for a third term in Congress. O'Connell, as a delegate, called on the Massachusetts Constitutional Convention in 1917 to make the judiciary subject to the initiative and referendum process, which ultimately could have led to the popular election of magistrates. His plea was unsuccessful.[23]

The question of access to formal legal education was a more serious point of contention between Irish Catholics and Yankee Protestants. Before Charles Eliot became Harvard president in 1869, anyone of "good moral character" and financial means could attend Harvard Law School. But Eliot, to quote one faculty member, turned everything over like a "flapjack." Concerned, as were many bar associations, about the inadequate training of young lawyers, he raised admission requirements, introduced a grading system, and expanded the course of study. Harvard Law School in 1893 decided to admit, without examination, undergraduates of certain select colleges; students enrolled in Catholic institutions such as Boston College, with few exceptions, were required to take entrance examinations. If accepted, they were designated "special" students and required to maintain grade averages twenty points higher than those of other students. Boston College Jesuits were infuriated by this arbitrary classification, which stigmatized their graduates with second-class status. Giving in to their vehement protests, Eliot rescinded this policy in 1898, only to reintroduce it shortly thereafter, and a battle ensued. [24]

Eliot justified his actions on the grounds that Boston College undergraduates had performed poorly at the Law School. All nine attending the school, he said in 1899, were "close to the lower borderline" in their classes. Earlier he had publicly criticized the Jesuits for clinging to a classical course of study that, he asserted, neglected the modern natural sciences and had remained almost unchanged for nearly four hundred years. In response, Father Timothy Brosnahan, in a thirty-two-page pamphlet, compared the course of instruction offered undergraduates at Jesuit institutions and at Harvard College. At a Jesuit school a student was required to divide his time equally among offerings in Latin, Greek, philosophy, English, mathematics, modern languages, and the natural sciences. This curriculum contrasted sharply, noted Brosnahan, with Eliot's elective system, which made it possible for an undergraduate to receive a bachelor's degree without taking any natural science courses. Criticizing Eliot for overemphasizing "individuality," Brosnahan insisted that young students needed intellectual guidance. [25]

If Eliot had been as concerned as he claimed to be about the inadequacy of Jesuit education, especially in the natural sciences, he might have concentrated his attention on the medical school, where a strong background in the sciences was more critical. It seemed odd that Harvard Law School was still tolerating the "gentleman's C" student from non-Catholic colleges until Eliot's retirement in 1909 and that Catholics were singled out for poor academic performance. The same man who defended parochial schools and praised certain Boston Irish politicians may have feared that Harvard-trained Irish lawyers, unlike Harvard-educated Irish physicians, could alter the commercial and financial world of Yankee Boston. And Eliot, a gentleman, scholar, and member of Boston's ruling elite, probably never lost sight of this possibility. [26]

After the Civil War, evening law schools had become an important avenue of social mobility for sons of immigrant working-class parents. In 1906 Gleason L. Archer, an enterprising young lawyer from Maine, founded the Suffolk School of Law in the living room of his home in the neighborhood of Roxbury. His evening torts and contracts classes were attended by Irish, Italian, Jewish, and Norwegian students. But Archer's dream of "uplifting" the students won little support from the members of Boston's legal establishment. Attempting to make attorneys of them, one remarked, was "like trying to turn cart horses into trotters." When Suffolk petitioned the Massachusetts State Legislature in 1912 for the right to grant degrees, the Yankee-dominated State Board of Education, the Boston Bar Association, and Harvard University argued that law schools like Suffolk tended to turn out second-rate lawyers and that there was already an oversupply of attorneys. A. Lawrence Lowell, President Eliot's successor at Harvard, gave unfavorable testimony before a legislative committee hearing arguments on the bill. Archer accused Harvard of trying to monopolize state legal education and called the university an "educational octopus." And in an emotional speech in the state legislature, Martin M. Lomasney, a renowned Irish politician from Boston's West End and self-styled "champion of the masses," exclaimed, "Don't let the lawyers of this body make a trust of legal education in Massachusetts." Lomasney and Archer saw their bill vetoed on two separate occasions by Governor Eugene N. Foss, a trustee of a rival evening law school, but, with the election of Governor David I. Walsh in 1914, the charter giving Suffolk degree granting powers was finally signed into law.[27]

The Irish encountered far less discrimination in the field of medicine, though it was also Yankee-dominated. In fact, Yankee physicians were instrumental in establishing and staffing numerous Catholic hospitals. Oliver Wendell Holmes of Harvard Medical School helped to promote the careers of promising Irish medical students like Michael Freebern Gavin. Gavin migrated to Boston in 1857 and worked in his in-laws' apothecary business, where he obtained a sound knowledge of medicines. Entering Harvard Medical School in 1861, he quickly won praise from Dr. Holmes as "an intelligent and very industrious student." With Holmes's assistance, the

Fig. 14. Michael Freebern Gavin (1844–1915), an eminent Boston Irish physician, in Civil War uniform.

twenty-year-old Gavin obtained a prized house residency at the newly opened Boston City Hospital in 1864. Following two years' study abroad, he returned to South Boston, where he entered private practice. He made thirty to forty house calls daily, never allowing his schedule to be upset by idle gossip with his patients. It was said that his driver could tell to the minute just how long to let his horse trot down the road on a cold day before turning the carriage around to meet Dr. Gavin emerging from the patient's house.[28]

It could be difficult for an Irish physician without Gavin's talents or connections to establish a satisfactory medical practice. Many advertised in order to attract patients. In 1848, Dr. Hodnett, a former resident of County Cork and a member of England's Royal College of Surgeons, notified *Pilot* readers that he specialized in the treatment of eye infection, fever, and complications caused by incompetent midwives. Dr. J. D. Walsh promised "honesty and propriety" in the treatment of all his patients, and Dr. Constantine B. O'Donnell, formerly of Dublin, was available at any hour for "urgent cases." A typical Irish physician studied at Harvard Medical School, practiced in a Boston neighborhood, and, to augment his regular income, served on the staff at one of Boston's Catholic hospitals or charitable institutions or as a medical examiner for insurance companies, schools, and fraternal organizations.[29]

Of the many Irish physicians participating in politics, chiefly as members of the Boston School Committee, three of the most politically prominent were William Aloysius Dunn, John George Blake, and George W. Galvin. Dunn served with distinction on the School Committee during the American Protective Association's crusade against Catholics and immigrants in the 1890s. John George Blake, a School Committeeman for sixteen years and the father of eleven children, championed military drill, manual training, and regular sanitation inspections of school facilities. Successful in real estate promotions and stock investments as well as in medicine, he was worth more than $100,000 at the time of his death. Dr. George Galvin worked as a railroad surgeon in the 1880s and became aware of the need for readily accessible medical facilities in the industrial sections of the city to provide emergency treatment for brakemen, teamsters, and machine workers. (The medical profession at that time saw little connection between immediate treatment and the likelihood of successful recovery.) Aided by employers who wished to minimize insurance claims and loss of manhours, Galvin became one of the founders of the Boston Emergency Hospital in 1891. Despite strong opposition from certain segments of the medical profession who viewed such experiments as a potential threat to their own private practices, Galvin in 1899 established another hospital which provided medical services to workers at a modest premium and at hours convenient to them. A political maverick, he ran unsuccessfully in 1902 as the Socialist party's candidate for mayor of Boston.[30]

Successful as they were, Irish doctors still had difficulty penetrating Boston's medical establishment. While constituting at least 12 percent of the medical profession in Boston in 1905, they were greatly underrepresented in such prestigious associations as the Boston Society for Medical Improvement. Founded in 1828 to promote social and intellectual exchange among its members, it was, as one Yankee member testified, "exclusive" and influential in controlling the "medical fortunes" of the community. Only 4 of its 278 members between 1865 and 1903 were Irish. The Massachusetts Medical Society usually admitted any qualified Irish physician as a general member, but only one of the 93 officers between 1865 and 1917 was Irish. Other coveted positions were inaccessible to Irish physicians. Of 519 doctors appointed to the Harvard Medical School faculty and staff between 1865 and 1917, only 16 were Irish, and only 5 of the 224 assigned over the same period to Massachusetts General Hospital were of Irish descent. Inbreeding and nepotism were in part responsible for the exclusion of Irish Catholics from these institutions and societies. To ensure that all physicians were given fair consideration, President Eliot fought unsuccessfully during the 1870s to have positions at Massachusetts General Hospital awarded on the basis of competitive examination rather than on the recommendations of hospital trustees. Dr. Gavin, refused a visiting staff position at the Brahmin-controlled Boston City Hospital in 1872, later complained to a friend that "he had always felt that he had more than sufficient grounds for feeling aggrieved." Denied what one Yankee physician called the "certain well-understood advantages" of being affiliated with a hospital like Massachusetts General, many Irish physicians, in addition, lacked the means to go abroad to study the latest developments in medical science. Without benefit of this additional knowledge or "the prospect of building up an honest fame" by being able to treat as many patients as did those assigned to major hospitals, few Irish doctors were able to advance to the top of their profession.[31]

One calling in which the Irish encountered no discrimination was the priesthood. The opening of Saint John's Seminary in Brighton in 1884 ended the practice of sending candidates for the priesthood to Paris, Montreal, or Baltimore. In comparison to some law and medical schools, entrance requirements to Saint John's were high: candidates generally had to complete the equivalent of two years of undergraduate study and pass examinations in Latin, English, and mathematics. The young seminarian, in cassock and biretta, was expected to master the virtues of "humility, unworldliness, industry, solitude and assiduous prayerfulness." Rising before sunrise, he said his prayers, tidied up his room, and went to Mass, followed by breakfast. He was thereafter kept busy with prayers, rosaries, spiritual readings, and examination of conscience as well as with classes on Canon Law, Church History, theology, and preaching. To develop humility and self-denial every seminarian took a turn serving in the dining hall and abstained from reading newspapers, smoking, or talking in the dormitory. The rector allowed his "Irish-American children in Christ" free time for ice skating, billiards, baseball, and family visits on Sunday.[32]

During their six-year stay at Saint John's, seminarians were evaluated on character, health, intelligence, attention to duty, and reading and preaching abilities. Students on certain days might be described by the rector as "pious," "well-bred," "cheerful," "capable," and "studious" and on other days as "docile," "weak-willed," "boyish," "obsequious," "self-centered," and "somewhat uncouth." In preaching or reading sermons the seminarians were criticized for poor organization, "monotonous" and "muffled" delivery, and "high-pitched," "shrill" voices. Seminarians sometimes balked at aspects of their highly regimented training, like lengthy spiritual readings at suppertime and hour-long meditations. Students criticized the practice of having to walk in large groups while off the seminary grounds. Some seminarians went a little too far: in 1909 a student returned "noisy" and "somewhat shaky" from a picnic, having consumed too much "liquor in the spirit of bravado." Expelled before the opening of fall classes, he pleaded for reinstatement but was told to first undergo a "period of trial in the world." He then went to New York, taught school, attended Mass, confession, and Communion regularly, and even took the pledge. Promising to study harder and use his talents to the "greater glory of Christ's Church," he reapplied for admission after one year but was again turned down. Those who made it beyond ordination were usually assigned to a local parish. If a young priest demonstrated leadership as a parish organizer or fund-raiser, he could be promoted to pastor within ten years. He was considered to have fulfilled his duties if his parishioners were neatly dressed, industrious, contributed regularly to the support of the parish school, avoided gossip, and remembered what he had said during his Sunday sermon.[33]

Public schooling had contributed to widespread literacy, which by the 1880s made America what one observer called "the land of the general reader." Newspaper publishers, to keep up with the tremendous demand for news and to reap soaring profits in advertising, expanded their staffs. By 1905, over one-fifth of approximately five hundred Boston journalists were Irish. Patrick Donahoe, who came to Boston in 1821, started his career in a printing shop and by 1839 had taken over the *Pilot*. Three decades later, he had increased the paper's circulation from 7,000 to over 100,000, which made him a man of considerable wealth and influence. As publisher of "the Irishman's Bible," as the *Pilot* was commonly known,

Fig. 15. Patrick Donahoe (1811–1901), publisher and editor of the "Irish-man's Bible," the Boston Pilot, *from 1839 to 1875. Note the crucifix around Donahoe's neck.*

he provided his fellow immigrants with information on naturalization procedures, missing relatives, and employment opportunities and shaped public opinion on political matters in the United States and Ireland. In support of Daniel O'Connell's Repeal movement of the 1840s, he appeared on Boston streets wearing a green coat and badge demanding "Repeal," and during the Know-Nothing movement in the 1850s, he attacked "the foul breath of Nativism." At first he sharply criticized abolitionists, fearing that emancipated Negroes would compete with Irish workers for jobs, but after the Civil War began, he personally helped recruit Irish regiments in the interest of preserving the Union. The Great Boston Fire of 1872 halted the *Pilot* presses; Donahoe tried to publish his newspaper on two other occasions but again was thwarted by fire. When his other banking, real estate, and shipping interests were hurt by the depression a year later, he imprudently used customers' deposits at a bank with which he was associated. Forced into bankruptcy, Donahoe, now sixty-five, sold his newspaper to Archbishop John Williams and John Boyle O'Reilly.[34]

Sentenced to an Australian penal colony in 1867 for plotting revolution against the British crown, O'Reilly escaped and made his way to Boston, where he was to become the city's first Irish folk hero. Donahoe employed him as a reporter and later as an editor, and almost immediately his poems and essays on racial and social injustice won praise. In his editorials O'Reilly deplored the exploitation of the workingman, declaring that corporations had "large pockets but no souls" and describing Andrew Carnegie as a "mock philanthropist" and Jay Gould and Cornelius Vanderbilt as "colossal robbers." Admired by Brahmins like Thomas Wentworth Higginson and Oliver Wendell Holmes, O'Reilly was invited to compose the appropriate verses for the dedication of Plymouth Rock in 1889.[35]

Boston Globe publisher Charles H. Taylor began in the 1870s to cater to the Irish interest in politics, labor, sports, and neighborhood events and was a major employer of Irish reporters. Galway-born Martin J. O'Brien started as an office boy at the *Globe* in 1887 and became a newsman reporting on the intrigues of "secret societies." Michael Curran covered the Irish Home Rule issue, and James O'Leary, "a lovable, big, smiling Irishman," was the *Globe*'s baseball expert. Thomas Evans commented on horse racing in his columns, "Hoof Prints" and "Stable Echoes." At the *Boston Post*, on downtown Boston's Newspaper Row, Daniel and Frederic O'Connell were part of what one grumbling newspaper veteran called the "damn" college crowd that was beginning to invade the field in the expectation of making it their profession. The O'Connells, when not attending classes at Harvard, covered the political beat in Boston.[36]

The question arises, in surveying Irishmen who attained status and wealth as grocers, liquor dealers, contractors, undertakers, lawyers, doctors, and journalists, why most Irishmen still found themselves in working-class occupations as late as World War I. Yankee bigotry was not the sole reason. A later immigrant group, the Jews, had to overcome similar prejudice in addition to a language barrier and still managed to outdistance the Irish in the professions and related white-collar jobs. While it involved considerable sacrifice for Irish parents to send their sons to institutions of higher education, such as Boston College or Harvard College—where the annual tuition in 1900 was $72 and $150, respectively—some found a way. Elizabeth O'Connell, the wife of an Irish plasterer, used the family's small savings to invest in real estate in Dorchester, reinvesting the money in other property, to finance part of her five sons' education. On one occasion her husband had to file for bankruptcy, and her children frequently had to withdraw temporarily from Boston College or Harvard to help augment the family income by working as newspaper reporters. She lived to see three of her sons become lawyers, another a veterinarian, and the youngest a well known sportswriter.[37]

One must suspect, however, that in many instances Irish parents acted as a cultural brake on the social aspirations of their children by drastically underestimating the importance of extended, formal education as a means of getting ahead.

Fig. 16. The O'Connell family—a Boston Irish success story. Arriving as immigrants in the 1860s, Mr. and Mrs. James O'Connell had five sons, three of whom went on to become lawyers, another a veterinarian, and the youngest a well known sportswriter.

Parochial school teachers publicly complained that some parents were "over-eager" to have their children quit school and start earning money. This tendency was prompted, not by abject poverty, the *Pilot* intimated in 1915, but by the shortsighted desire to improve their modest but not uncomfortable standard of living. Noting that Irish Americans lacked the "indomitable passion for improvement" characteristic of groups like the Jews, the *Republic*, a Boston Irish weekly, attributed the slow progress of the Irish to "complacency" and a preoccupation with having a "dandy time." Many Irish even neglected the library as an opportunity for educational self-improvement: in 1909, there was a smaller percentage of library card holders in the heavily Irish wards—thirteen and nineteen—than in ward eight, where many of Boston's Jewish immigrants lived.[38]

The progress of the Irish was hampered most of all by their

phenomenal success in politics and the Boston labor movement. Eager to win elections and to satisfy their supporters' impulse to "make men's pay," the Irish politician channeled generations of Irish into secure but financially dead-end jobs as city clerks, firefighters, policemen, and utility and transit employees. (At the turn of the century one of every three Irish families in the North and West Ends was estimated to have someone employed through political patronage.) John F. Cronan, a Boston attorney, referring to the large number of young Irishmen holding municipal jobs, noted that they were "stalled for life, as they attain the poor maximum salary in a few years, and then, with no chance of advancement, stagnate for the balance of their lives." Neither the public nor the parochial school, in emphasizing individual risk taking and self-help, had been able to counter the influence of fathers discussing the merits of union employment and steady-paying jobs on the city payroll. It was this preoccupation with security that prevented more Irish from becoming moderately successful as businessmen, doctors, and lawyers, who were considered financially and socially superior to city clerks or street inspectors.[39]

NOTES

1. For information on the economic life of nineteenth-century Boston see Justin Winsor, ed., *The Memorial History of Boston, 1630–1880*, 4 vols. (Boston: 1880–81), 4:69–234; Frederic Cople Jaher, "The Boston Brahmins in the Age of Industrial Capitalism," in *The Age of Industrialism in America*, ed. Jaher (New York: 1968), pp. 189–94; Oscar Handlin, *Boston's Immigrants, A Study in Acculturation*, rev. and enl. ed. (Cambridge, Mass.: 1959), pp. 54–87; Arthur Mann, *Yankee Reformers in the Urban Age* (Cambridge, Mass: 1954), pp. 1–23.

2. Handlin, *Boston's Immigrants*, pp. 62, 70–72.

3. Abner and Frank Forbes, *"Our First Men:" A Calendar of Wealth, Fashion and Gentility* (Boston: 1846), p. 16; Abner Forbes, *The Rich Men of Massachusetts* (Boston: second ed., 1852), pp. iv, 20; James Bernard Cullen, ed., *The Story of the Irish in Boston* (Boston: 1889), pp. 406–8; Sister Ann St. Joseph Murphy, S.N.D., "Andrew Carney, the Boston Philanthropist" (Master's thesis, Boston College, 1958), pp. 1–16; Robert H. Lord, John E. Sexton, and Edward T. Harrington, *History of the Archdiocese of Boston*, 3 vols. (New York: 1944), 2:343, 467.

4. Handlin, *Boston's Immigrants*, pp. 65, 250, Table XIII; Robert Ernst, *Immigrant Life in New York City, 1825–1863* (New York: 1949), pp. 86, 87; Wilfred J. Mailhoit, *Mailhoit's Modern Adviser to Grocers* (Boston: 1919), pp. 12–17, 37–41.

5. R. G. Dun & Company, credit ledgers, *Massachusetts Volumes* 76:48, 49; 73:175; 78:190, Baker Library, Manuscript Division and Archives, Harvard University Graduate School of Business Administration; Clyde and Sally Griffen, *Natives and Newcomers: The Ordering of Opportunity in Mid-Nineteenth-Century Poughkeepsie* (Cambridge, Mass.: 1978), p. 131; Robert A. Silverman, *Law and Urban Growth: Civil Litigation in the Boston Trial Courts, 1880–1900* (Princeton, N.J.: 1981), pp. 53 55.

6. Elizabeth Hafkin Pleck, *Black Migration and Poverty, Boston 1865–1900* (New York: 1979), Table V-8, p. 154; James D. Norris, *R. G. Dun & Co., 1841–1900: The Development of Credit-Reporting in the Nineteenth Century* (Westport, Conn.: 1978), pp. xvii, 87, 125–28, 164; Peter R. Decker, *Fortunes and Failures: White-Collar Mobility in Nineteenth-Century San Francisco* (Cambridge, Mass.: 1978), pp. 99–101, 257, 258; David Gerber, "Ethnics, Enterprise, and Middle Class Formation: Using the Dun and Bradstreet Collection for Research in Ethnic History," *The Immigration History Newsletter* 12 (May 1980):2, 3, 6; Dun & Co., *Mass. Vols.* 77:238, 260; 76:143, 233; 77:59. The Baker Library at the Harvard University Graduate School of Business Administration, Boston, has more than 2,500 volumes of R. G. Dun & Co. credit ledgers. For the purpose of this study, the author contrasted the treatment of 100 randomly selected credit seekers bearing non-Irish names with those of 100 having Irish surnames. Before consulting these reports, one should read James H. Madison, "The Credit Reports of R. G. Dun & Co. as Historical Sources," *Historical Methods Newsletter* 8, no. 4 (September 1975):128–31; J. W. Lozier, "Uses of Nineteenth Century Credit Reports: A Researcher's Review of the Dun and Bradstreet Collection, 1845–1890," manuscript, Archives collection, Baker Library. Also, because agents frequently used abbreviations and codes, such as " + " to mean "and," the author, for the sake of clarity, has taken the liberty of substituting words spelled in their entirety.

7. Stanley K. Schultz, *The Culture Factory: Boston Public Schools, 1789–1860* (New York: 1973), p. 239; Robert A. Woods, ed., *Americans in Process* (Boston: 1902), pp. 106, 107; Roger Lane, *Policing the City, Boston, 1822–1885* (Cambridge, Mass.: 1967), pp. 42–45; Dun & Co., *Mass. Vols.* 76:86; 77:205, 211; 73:236; *Boston Pilot*, 27 December 1862; Gallus Thomann, "The Brewing Industry in New England," in *The New England States*, ed. William T. Davis, 4 vols. (Boston: 1897), 4:2290–92; Dun & Co., *Mass. Vols.* 86:180; Geoffrey Blodgett, *The Gentle Reformers: Massachusetts Democrats in the Cleveland Era* (Cambridge, Mass.: 1966), p. 143; *Mass. Vols.* 74:212, 225, 1L; 77:146; John J. Toomey and Edward P. B. Rankin, *History of South Boston* (Boston: 1901), pp. 527, 529; *Mass. Vols.* 67:216, A114, A156; *Boston Evening Transcript*, 14 September 1921.

8. Lane, *Policing the City*, pp. 163, 164; Dun & Co., *Mass. Vols.* 76:51; Cullen, *The Story of the Irish in Boston* (rev. ed., 1893), pp. 629, 567; *Mass. Vols.* 79:201; John Henry Cutler, *"Honey Fitz": Three Steps to the White House—The Life and Times of John F. (Honey Fitz) Fitzgerald* (Indianapolis, Ind.: 1962), pp. 9, 72, 73.

9. Charles Phillips Huse, *The Financial History of Boston from May 1, 1882 to January 31, 1909* (Cambridge, Mass.: 1916), Appendix I, 349–51.

10. Charles S. Damrell, *A Half Century of Boston's Building* (Boston: 1895), pp. 463, 418–20, 493; Sam B. Warner, Jr., *Streetcar Suburbs: The Process of Growth in Boston, 1870–1900* (Cambridge, Mass.: 1962), p. 127; *Boston Evening Transcript*, 22 October 1900; *Boston Pilot*, 27 October 1900; *Boston Post*, 21 October 1900; *Boston Pilot*, 13 December 1919; newspaper clippings of Charles Logue in author's possession.

11. Toomey and Rankin, *History of South Boston*, p. 515; Dun & Co., *Mass. Vols.* 80:176, 177, 366; *Boston Evening Transcript*, 12 November 1901; *Annual Report of the Superintendent of Streets for the Year 1887*, city document no. 23 (Boston: 1888), pp. 91, 101.

12. Massachusetts Bureau of Statistics of Labor, *Census of the Commonwealth of Massachusetts, 1905*, 4 vols. (Boston: 1908–10), vol. 2, *Occupations and Defective Social and Physical Condition*, p. 154; *Boston Globe*, 28 March 1922; Richard J. Whalen, *The Founding Father: The Story of Joseph P. Kennedy* (New York: 1964), p. 28; Huse, *The Financial History of Boston*, pp. 236, 237; *The Finance Commission of the City of Boston*, 3 vols. (Boston: 1908–9), vol. 3, Appendices.

13. *The Finance Commission of the City of Boston* 1:462–70, 480.

14. *First Annual Report of the Board of Registration in Embalming for the Year 1906* (Boston: 1907), pp. 3–5; Massachusetts Bureau of Statistics of Labor, *Census of the Commonwealth of Massachusetts, 1905*, vol. 2, *Occupations and Defective Social and Physical Condition*, pp. 146–47; Robert W. Habenstein and William M. Lamers, *The History of American Funeral Directing* (Milwaukee, Wis.: rev. ed., 1962), pp. 399–409, 473, 474, 477; Curtis F. Callaway, *The Art of Funeral Directing: A Practical Manual on Modern Funeral Directing Methods* (Chicago, Ill.: 1928), pp. 15–19, 24–39, 61–66, 93–103. This author was able to ascertain the previous occupations of thirty Boston Irish undertakers by checking Dun & Co. ledgers; newspapers; Cullen, *The Story of the Irish in Boston* (1889, 1893 editions); Toomey and Rankin, *History of South Boston*; and Albert P. Langtry, ed., *Metropolitan Boston, A Modern History*, 5 vols. (New York: 1929).

15. William H. Porter, Jr., "Some Sociological Notes on a Century of Change in the Funeral Business," *Sociological Symposium* (Fall 1968), 1:39, 41; Cullen, *The Story of the Irish in Boston* (1893), p. 457; Richard Herndon, *Boston of Today: A Glance at its History and Characteristics* (Boston: 1892), p. 365; Langtry, ed., *Metropolitan Boston*, V:217, 218; *Boston Evening Transcript*, 7 August 1895.

16. Dun & Co., *Mass. Vols.* 74:200; 90:343; Suffolk County Probate Court Records, Boston, Massachusetts, docket number 116933; Toomey and Rankin, *History of South Boston*, pp. 533, 524.

17. *Sacred Heart Review*, 22 February 1890; Dun & Co., *Mass. Vols.* 77:370; ledgers of John D. Fallon, in the possession of Ronald K. West, proprietor, Brady and Fallon Funeral Home, Jamaica Plain, Mass.

18. William T. Davis, *Bench and Bar of the Commonwealth of Massachusetts*, 2 vols. (Boston: 1895), 1:429; Massachusetts Bureau of Statistics of Labor, *Census of the Commonwealth of Massachusetts, 1905*, vol. 2, *Occupations and Defective Social and Physical Condition*, pp. 132, 133; Hollis R. Bailey, *Attorneys and Their Admission to the Bar in Massachusetts* (Boston: 1907), pp. 39–46, 65–78; Robert Grant, "Bench and Bar in Massachusetts (1889–1929)," in *Commonwealth History of Massachusetts*, ed. Albert Bushnell Hart, 5 vols. (New York: 1927–30), 5:103, 104. How easy it was to become a lawyer in Boston was attested to by Charles Francis Adams. After some "desultory

reading" in a law office, Adams in 1850 went to see his neighbor and family friend, Judge George T. Bigelow, and requested an examination. He was invited to the judge's courtroom, where he was handed a letter-size piece of paper with a few questions scribbled on it. Adams answered some of them but later confessed to knowing "absolutely nothing" about the rest. Meeting the judge a few days later at a railroad station, Adams was informed he had passed. Excited as any young lawyer would be, he nevertheless noted that he was no more fit "than a child" to be a lawyer (Lawrence M. Friedman, *A History of American Law* ([New York: 1973], p. 565); *Boston Pilot*, 9 February 1850 and 5 January 1867.

19. Davis, *Bench and Bar*, 1:450, 451, 511, 512; Joseph Smith, *Thomas J. Gargan, A Memorial* (Boston: 1910), pp. 17, 18, 59, 61; *City of Boston Tax Assessor's Records*, 1900; Conrad Reno, *Memoirs of the Judiciary and the Bar of New England for the Nineteenth Century* (Boston: 1901), vol. 1, part 2, pp. 66–68; 2:659–61; Blodgett, *Gentle Reformers*, pp. 144, 145; Katherine E. Conway and Mabel Ward Cameron, *Charles Francis Donnelly, A Memoir* (New York: 1909), pp. 10–12, 19, 20, 31–225, 226, 227, 235, 236, 238, 249.

20. Conway and Cameron, *Donnelly*, pp. 232–34; *Holy Cross Purple* 8 (May 1899): 344; ibid. 23 (January 1911):275; ibid. 8 (May 1899):345–50.

21. For political activities of Irish lawyers the author relied on biographical information found chiefly in Cullen, *The Story of the Irish in Boston* (Boston: 1889),pp. 285–300; Davis, *Bench and Bar*, 2 vols.; Reno, *Memoirs of the Judiciary*, 2 vols.; *General Alumni Catalogue of Boston University*, compiled by W. J. Maxwell (Boston: 1918), pp. 151–236; Law folder and docket book of Joseph F. O'Connell, in author's possession. Of 88 attorneys hired by one State Street law office between 1865 and 1917, only two were of Irish descent. See surnames in Albert Boyden, *Ropes-Gray, 1865–1940* (Boston: 1942), pp. 203–15.

22. James Willard Hurst, *The Growth of American Law: The Law Makers* (Boston: 1950), pp. 128–46; Friedman, *A History of American Law*, pp. 323–39; Commonwealth of Massachusetts, *Report of Committee on the Inferior Courts of the County of Suffolk* (Boston, 11 January 1912), 5, 6; Davis, *Bench and Bar*, 1:596; Reno, *Memoirs of the Judiciary*, 2:495, 496; *Holy Cross Purple* 3 (June 1896):49, 50; ibid. 27 (December 1914):163, 164; ibid. 29 (April 1917): 429–31; *The Massachusetts Lawyers Diary for 1917* (Cambridge, Mass.: 1916), pp. 19, 20.

23. For a list of associate justices of the Superior Court between 1859 and 1913 see *Massachusetts Law Quarterly* 44 (July 1959):123–25; for the justices of the Supreme Court, see Massachusetts Bar Association, *The Supreme Judicial Court of Massachusetts 1692–1942* (Boston: 1943?), pp. 51, 52; *Massachusetts Law Quarterly* 3 (May 1918):298, 290, 299–301. The probability of an Irish Catholic lawyer winning admission to the Boston Bar Association was about as good as an immigrant's chance of becoming president of the Society of Mayflower Descendants. At the turn of the century the Irish constituted roughly 20 percent of the city's legal profession, but only 3 percent of the Bar Association's 811 members were of Irish extraction (*Boston Republic*, 29 October 1904). For information on stratification within the Massachusetts legal profession see Gerard W. Gawalt, *The Promise of Power: The Emergence of the Legal Profession in Massachusetts, 1760–1840* (Westport, Conn.: 1979).

24. Hugh Hawkins, *Between Harvard and America: The Educational Leadership of*

Charles W. Eliot (New York: 1972), pp. 58–61, 186, 187; Henry K. Beecher and Mark D. Altschule, *Medicine at Harvard: The First Three Hundred Years* (Hanover, N.H.: 1977), p. 88; Friedman, *A History of American Law*, pp. 525–38; David R. Dunigan, *A History of Boston College* (Milwaukee, Wis.: 1947), pp. 168–77.

25. Marcia Graham Synnott, *A Social History of Admissions Policies at Harvard, Yale, and Princeton, 1900–1930*, 2 vols. (Ann Arbor, Mich.: University Microfilms International, 1974), 1:236–40; Hawkins, *Between Harvard and America*, pp. 187, 188; Timothy Brosnahan, S.J., "President Eliot and Jesuit Colleges," reprint from the *Sacred Heart Review*, 13 January 1900, pp. 11, 12, 19–21, 25, 26, 30, 31.

26. Arthur E. Sutherland, *The Law at Harvard: A History of Ideas and Men, 1817–1967* (Cambridge, Mass.: 1967), p. 221; Hawkins, *Between Harvard and America*, pp. 184, 185, 189. For Eliot's relationship with the medical school see Beecher and Altschule, *Medicine at Harvard*, pp. 85–125, and for an interpretation favorable to Eliot's point of view see Synnott's *The Half-Opened Door: Discrimination and Admissions at Harvard, Yale, and Princeton, 1900–1970* (Westport, Conn.: 1979), pp. 41–43.

27. Friedman, *A History of American Law*, pp. 537–38; Jerold S. Auerbach, *Unequal Justice: Lawyers and Social Change in Modern America* (New York: 1976), pp. 97, 98; Gleason L. Archer, *Fifty Years of Suffolk University* (n.p., 5 April 1956), pages unnumbered; Archer, *The Educational Octopus* (Boston: 1915), pp. 21, 48–50, 77, 78, 173–78, 188, 193, 194, 207, 211, 218–20, 246, 272, 277, 278.

28. *Michael Freebern Gavin, A Biography*, edited by his son (Cambridge, Mass.: 1915), pp. 11, 14, 15, 20, 27–35; Henry R. Viets, "The Resident House Staff at the Opening of the Boston City Hospital in 1864," *Journal of the History of Medicine and Allied Sciences* 14 (April 1959):183–85; *Boston Medical and Surgical Journal* 172 (3 June 1915):840. For information on the extensive humanitarian endeavors of Yankee physicians see Morris J. Vogel, *The Invention of the Modern Hospital: Boston 1870–1930* (Chicago: 1980).

29. *Boston Pilot*, 16 September 1848, 2 September 1854, 12 January 1850. This generalization is based on biographical information found on some sixty Irish Catholic physicians in Cullen, *The Story of the Irish in Boston* (Boston: 1889), pp. 303–7; Thomas Francis Harrington, M.D., *The Harvard Medical School: A History, Narrative and Documentary*, 3 vols. (New York: 1905), 3:1476–1648; *General Alumni Catalogue of Boston University*, pp. 237–71; and obituaries in the *Boston Medical and Surgical Journal*.

30. Lord, Sexton, and Harrington, *History of the Archdiocese*, 3:377, 378, 403; *Boston College Stylus* 13 (January 1899):7; George W. Gay, M.D., "John George Blake, M.D.," *Boston Medical and Surgical Journal* 178 (March 28, 1918):446–48; ibid. (11 April 1918):514; Cullen, *The Story of the Irish in Boston* (1893), pp. 422–26, 412; John Bapst Blake, "John George Blake," in *American Medical Biographies*, eds. Howard A. Kelly, M.D. and Walter L. Burrage, M.D. (Baltimore, Md.: 1920), pp. 110, 111; William B. Atkinson, M.D., ed., *A Biographical Dictionary of Contemporary American Physicians and Surgeons* (Philadelphia: 1880), pp. 420, 421; Suffolk County Probate Court Records, docket number 181687; George W. Galvin, M.D., "The Necessity of an Emergency Hospital in the Business District of Boston," *Boston Medical and Surgical Journal* 124 (February 5, 1891):134–36; *Boston Globe*, 17 August 1928; *Boston Post*, 17 August 1928; Vogel, *The Modern Hospital*, pp. 47–57, 145, footnote no. 76; *First*

Annual Report of the Boston Emergency Hospital, July 1, 1892 (Boston: 1892), pp. 5–9, Massachusetts State Library, State House, Boston; *Report of the Boston Emergency Hospital from November 15, 1894 to November 15, 1895,* pp. 4, 5, 7; Henry F. Bedford, *Socialism and the Workers in Massachusetts 1886–1912* (Amherst, Mass.: 1966), p. 168.

31. Massachusetts Bureau of Statistics of Labor, *Census of the Commonwealth of Massachusetts, 1905,* vol. 2, *Occupations and Defective Social and Physical Condition,* pp. 132–33; J. G. Mumford, M.D., "The Story of the Boston Society for Medical Improvement," *Boston Medical and Surgical Journal* 144 (14 March 1901):249; *Constitution and By-Laws of the Boston Society for Medical Improvement, With a List of the Officers and Members, Past and Present* (Boston: 1905), pp. 23–27, Francis A. Countway Library of Medicine, Boston Medical Library–Harvard Medical Library, Boston; Walter L. Burrage, M.D., *A History of the Massachusetts Medical Society* (Norwood, Mass.: 1923), pp. 462–67. The figures on the Harvard University Medical School were arrived at by checking the surnames of faculty found in Harrington, *Harvard Medical School,* 3:1358–75, and the Harvard Medical School catalogues between 1904 and 1917; Frederic A. Washburn, M.D., *The Massachusetts General Hospital: Its Development, 1900–1935* (Boston: 1939), pp. 589–604. For the early formation of a Yankee medical and cultural elite see Ronald Story, *The Forging of an Aristocracy: Harvard & the Boston Upper Class, 1800–1870* (Middletown, Conn.: 1980), pp. 10–12, 16, 18, 19, 160–62, 173, 174; Vogel, *The Modern Hospital,* pp. 17–22, 29, 30, 86.

32. Lord, Sexton, and Harrington, *History of the Archdiocese,* 2:41; ibid., 3:57–61; John E. Sexton and Arthur J. Riley, *History of Saint John's Seminary, Brighton* (Boston: 1945), pp. 23, 27, 40, 57–60, 65, 69, 73–75, 150–52; *Holy Cross Purple* 9 (November 1899):184–89.

33. Sexton and Riley, *Saint John's Seminary,* pp. 73, 74, 86, 94; *St. John's Boston Ecclesiastical Seminary Report of Students* (1908–10), records of Saint John's Seminary, deposited at the Archdiocese of Boston Archives, Brighton, Mass., hereafter cited as A.B.A.; Rev. Francis P. Havey to Archbishop William O'Connell, 13 July 1910, O'Connell to Havey, 19 July 1910, Michael J. O'Keefe to O'Connell, 27 June 1910, records of Saint John's Seminary, A.B.A.; Donna Merwick, *Boston Priests, 1848–1910, A Study of Social and Intellectual Change* (Cambridge, Mass.: 1973), pp. 89, 90; *Boston Pilot,* 26 January, 2 February 1867.

34. Arthur Meier Schlesinger, *The Rise of the City, 1878–1898* (New York: 1938), pp. 160–71, 185, 195, 196, 201; Massachusetts Bureau of Statistics of Labor, *Census of the Commonwealth of Massachusetts, 1905,* vol. 2, *Occupations and Defective Social and Physical Condition,* p. 132; Mary Alphonsine Frawley, S.S.J., *Patrick Donahoe* (Washington, D.C.: 1946), pp. 4, 12, 20, 21, 31, 32, 54, 79, 80, 122–27, 137–39, 177, 185–87, 202, 206–10, 212, 213, 215, 217–19, 222, 241–44; Dun & Co., *Mass. Vols.* 69:418; Francis Robert Walsh, *The Boston Pilot: A Newspaper for the Irish Immigrant, 1829–1908* (Ann Arbor, Mich.: University Microfilms International, 1969), pp. 43–127.

35. Mann, *Yankee Reformers,* pp. 27–29, 35, 37–39; Walsh, *A Newspaper for the Irish Immigrant,* pp. 198, 200.

36. Louis M. Lyons, *Newspaper Story: One Hundred Years of the Boston Globe* (Cambridge, Mass.: 1971), pp. 15, 31, 36, 37, 47, 48, 60, 63, 82–85; George P. Anderson, *A Souvenir Portfolio of the Boston Globe* (Boston: 1899), pages unnumbered; Michael

Schudson, *Discovering the News: A Social History of American Newspapers* (New York: 1978), pp. 68–70; folders of Daniel T. and Frederic O'Connell, both in author's possession. For other biographical information on Irish journalists, see Cullen, *The Story of the Irish in Boston* (1889), pp. 311–35.

37. Stephan Thernstrom, *The Other Bostonians: Poverty and Progress in the American Metropolis 1880–1970* (Cambridge, Mass.: 1973), pp. 135–38, 161, 163, 186; *The Harvard University Catalogue, 1900–1901* (Cambridge, Mass.: 1901), p. 528; *Catalogue of the Officers and Students of Boston College, 1900–1901* (n.p., 1901), p. 31; O'Connell Family Records, in author's possession. Law or medical school admission requirements, like costs, were not prohibitive. A student without a high school diploma, as late as 1900, could gain admission to day law schools such as Boston University by passing an entrance examination. Admission requirements at Boston University and Tufts Medical Schools were comparably simple. *Boston University Year Book XXVIII* (Boston: 1901), pp. 136, 146, 147, 160, 161, 178; Abraham Flexner, *Medical Education in the United States and Canada* (New York: 1910), pp. 240, 241.

38. "Report of the Supervisor of Schools on First Official Visit, January 1898 to January 1899: Archdiocese of Boston Parochial Schools," p. 19, deposited at the Archdiocesan Office of Catholic Schools, Boston; "Principles of Catholic Faith and Piety: How Best Inculcated in Our Schools," by a Sister of Charity, *Report of the Proceedings and Addresses of the 6th Annual Meeting of the Catholic Educational Association*, 6 (November 1909):396; *Boston Pilot*, 19 June 1915; *Boston Republic*, 6 April and 1 June 1907, 27 February 1904; I arrived at the conclusion regarding library users by cross-referencing the *Fifty-Seventh Annual Report of the Trustees of the Public Library of the City of Boston, 1908–1909* (Boston: 1909), p. 71 with United States Department of Commerce, Bureau of the Census, *Thirteenth Census of the United States, Taken in the Year 1910, II, Population, 1910* (Washington, D.C.: 1913), p. 890.

39. Robert A. Woods, ed., *Americans in Process* (Boston: 1902), p. 121; John F. Cronan, "The Progress of the Celt in Boston," *Boston Republic*, 22 February 1896, 27 February 1904. In succeeding at politics, the Irish, Thernstrom rightly suggests, seized "one kind of opportunity *at the expense of other opportunities*" (*The Other Bostonians*, p. 167).

5

The Irish at Leisure

The Hibernian is first, last and always a social being.

An observation by Boston social workers, 1902

The Irish need to escape discrimination and to survive as an
ethnic group was evident in their leisure and social activities:
just as they had created their own parochial schools and charitable institutions, they developed their own forms of entertainment. Devising leisure activities, like caring for the sick
and educating the young, was a natural function of the parish
church. Church picnics on hot summer days, featuring games
and dancing with music by Irish pipers, provided a respite for
tenement dwellers. A Roxbury parish organized athletic
teams, drama groups, and a marching band renowned for its
"manly appearance." The parish's Saint Alphonsus Association, providing "rational amusement" for young men over
eighteen years of age, had a library, a gymnasium, a bowling
alley, a billiard room, an auditorium for lectures and stage
productions, and a boathouse on the Charles River that served
hundreds of canoeists and rowers during the summer.[1]

Irish militia companies appeared regularly at parish functions, civic ceremonies, and parades. Like their countrymen in
New York and San Francisco, the Boston Irish banded together in the desire for companionship, recreation, and, in
their most quixotic moments, to hone their martial skills for
the day they would return to Erin's shores to liberate her by
force from John Bull's grip. Dressed in "warlike parapher-
nalia" and carrying rifles and "other implements of destruc-

Fig. 17. Suspected by nativist Yankees of harboring Jesuit spies within their ranks and of serving as advance guards for the impending invasion of America by the Pope, Irish militia companies like the Columbian Artillery were forced to disband during the Know-Nothing hysteria of the 1850s.

tion," the companies, after a public appearance, frequently adjourned to the Merchants' Exchange Hotel, where the Irish proprietor satisfied their thirst and appetite "with the richest viands of the season."[2]

Irish militia companies came under severe attack during the Know-Nothing era of the 1850s. Nativist Yankees suspected them of harboring Jesuit spies and of serving as advance guards for the impending papal invasion of America. They were also disliked for walking off repeatedly with first-place prizes in drill contests. Conscious that nativists were becoming uneasy over the spectacle of "Paddies" parading through the streets of Boston with "*real* swords and guns," the *Pilot* in 1853 tried to counsel the militia companies in a series of articles entitled "Soldiers." Only those willing to become naturalized citizens should be allowed into the ranks, it declared diplomatically. Good officers and drill instructors well versed in military discipline and "real soldiering" would prevent a unit from "going to the dogs" or from having its reputation tarnished by intoxicated members parading "in a very equivocal state." New units were urged to name themselves after George Washington or Alexander Hamilton, who, in contrast to Thomas Jefferson, were considered "conservative." The *Pilot*'s efforts were in vain: in 1853 the Know-Nothings succeeded in dissolving Irish militia companies with impeccably "American and conservative" names.[3]

The Irish wake was a form of therapeutic recreation that helped the bereaved to cope with the loss of a loved one. Rooted in pre-Christian Ireland, this custom was notorious for its merrymaking, prompted by the belief that elaborate celebrations were necessary in order to placate the deceased and to prevent evil spirits from entering the body. With the corpse the focus of attention, mourners, as a way of reaffirming their own existence as living, breathing mortals, abandoned themselves in drink and song, while women experienced in the ancient ritual of keening chanted the virtues of the deceased in shrill, haunting voices. Not until 1849, when hundreds of Irish perished during the cholera epidemic, did wakes come under close public scrutiny. The *Pilot*, anxious to protect the Irish image within Yankee Boston, condemned the "feasting and night-watching" as "useless customs."[4]

Professional boxing, like the Irish wake, was never fully accepted by Yankees or by Irishmen sensitive to outside opinion. *Donahoe's Magazine*, embarrassed by the post–Civil War domination of the fight game by the Irish, featured articles denouncing it as a form of "human butchery" supported chiefly by a "worthless, gambling class of loafers" who patronized saloons, poolrooms, and other "gilded haunts." In 1888, when John Boyle O'Reilly published a book extolling pugilism, the magazine sharply reprimanded him for endorsing such a "barbarous" pastime and insinuated that he was catering to popular tastes for pecuniary reasons.[5]

Such criticism did not faze O'Reilly, and he, Mayor Hugh O'Brien, and thousands of other Boston Irishmen continued to enjoy boxing. John L. Sullivan was America's first legendary sports hero. Born in Roxbury in 1858, Sullivan attended college briefly and worked at odd jobs before stumbling upon his calling one evening in 1877. Attending a performance at a local opera house where boxers put on exhibitions betweeen regular shows, he accepted the challenge of one fighter to take on anyone in the house. After sending his adversary flying into the orchestra pit with a mighty right blow to the head, the brawny nineteen-year-old strode to the edge of the stage and addressed the audience: "My name's John L. Sullivan, and I can lick any sonofabitch alive!"[6]

Other victories soon followed, and, with the shrewd coaching of his new trainer and promoter, William Muldoon, Sullivan quickly rose to national prominence by defeating Paddy Ryan for the world heavyweight championship in 1882. Though some accused him of being a bully, a drunkard, and a wife beater, Sullivan, oblivious to middle-class Victorian proprieties, appealed to self-made Irish Americans, and more than 3,000 Bostonians turned out in August 1887 to honor him with a $10,000 belt adorned with diamonds, gold, and emblems of Ireland and the United States. In 1889 the easygoing "Boston Strong Boy" won a bruising, bare-knuckle victory over Jake Kilrain in seventy-five rounds. Three years later, he traveled to New Orleans to defend his title against a soft-spoken "dude" from the West Coast named Jim Corbett. Sullivan was in his thirties and overweight. Breathing "like a huge porpoise," he was an easy target for the quick-hitting Corbett, who pummeled him into submission in twenty-one rounds. Many newspapers welcomed the downfall of the "idol of the barrooms," but in Boston there was only the "weeping and gnashing of teeth" among Sullivan's backers, as they blamed his defeat on old age, poor coaching, and "fast" living. Sullivan, who had feared his supporters would abandon him, was greeted by hundreds on his return to Boston. He spent his last days as an actor and as a temperance lecturer.[7]

A Galway native who got his start in Boston's entertainment world as an end man in minstrel shows, Patrick Sarsfield

Fig. 18. John L. Sullivan (1858–1918), twelve years after he lost his heavyweight title, with baseball star Jimmy Collins.

Gilmore became the greatest promoter of his day. Having composed the popular Civil War ballad, "When Johnny Comes Marching Home," as an army bandmaster, he considered it his mission in life to commemorate the restoration of peace and prosperity by staging "the grandest Musical Festival the world had ever known" in Boston in the summer of 1869. He persuaded businessmen, newspaper editors, and other "solid men" of Boston to fund the construction of a colosseum that could accommodate 50,000 people and the purchase of a gigantic organ and a drum that measured nearly twenty feet in diameter. The week-long festival featured a 1,000-piece orchestra and a chorus of 10,000 and attracted even President Ulysses S. Grant. Criticism for lowering musical standards with such "monster concerts" could hardly deter such a man. In 1872, he imported Johann Strauss, the "king of waltz-

makers," for another extravaganza, which also lured
thousands of Irish with old melodies played by a band from
Dublin.[8]

Many considered nineteenth-century Boston to be "the best
show town in the country," and the so-called stage Irishman
was rivaling the happy-go-lucky, watermelon-loving Negro,
the conniving Yankee trader, and the tall tale-telling western
frontiersman as the traditional butt of American humor. Usually named Pat, Paddy, or Teague, he spoke with a heavy
brogue and wore knee britches, a tall hat, and a ragged coat.
His props included a shillelagh, a clay pipe, and a whiskey
bottle, and his stock-in-trade was his gift of the blarney, his
inflated oratory, a propensity for fighting and drinking, and
inexhaustible wit and humor in the face of adversity. Attract-
ing the general public and nostalgic Irishmen, melodramas
and farces like *The Irish Free Lover*, *The Irishman's Shanty*, and
The Exiles of Erin were tremendous box office successes in
Boston. *Pilot* editor Patrick Donahoe refused to review such
productions and advised his readers to attend lectures instead.
Even Dion Boucicault, the Dublin-born playwright and actor
who was acclaimed in some circles as the "Irish Shakespeare,"
was criticized for perpetuating the "stage Irishman."[9]

As the Irish advanced economically and politically, their
stage image also improved, and writers of the popular drama
caricatured the newly arrived Jews and Italians instead. Revel-
ing in the heroic struggles of Irish peasants against oppressive
landlords, and laughing good-naturedly at productions that
parodied the difficulties of unexpected wealth and political
power, the Irish were confounded when John Millington
Synge's *The Playboy of the Western World* premiered in Boston
in 1911. The play, which provoked riots at the Abbey Theatre
in Dublin, is set in a small village in County Mayo, where a
stranger, Christy Mahon, has thrown the local inhabitants
into a frenzy by asserting that he has murdered his father.
After using religious expressions such as "Oh, glory be to
God!" to indicate their initial shock, the villagers soon take a
liking to this rogue, who has supposedly liberated himself
from the yoke of parental authority and defied civilized soci-

ety. Infatuated with his new heroic status, Mahon is caught off guard by the sudden appearance of his father. In an effort to regain his popularity, he tries to kill the old man but fails, and then, by a curious turn of events, he ultimately reconciles his differences with his "da."[10]

The Boston Irish failed to appreciate Synge's insight into human nature and lashed out at the play as an attempt by an Anglo-Irishman to demean the Irish character and to resurrect the stage Irishman. Michael J. Jordan, a past president of the Charitable Irish Society, claimed the play was "gross," "vulgar," "demoralizing," and "a glorification of murder." A priest with a "profound knowledge of the Irish character and language," sent by the *Pilot* to review the production, objected to religious expressions coming from the "lips of ruffians and murderers" and concluded that the play was an outright "insult to the Irish race." Under pressure from Irish organizations to ban the production, Mayor John F. Fitzgerald sent the city censor to study the play and on his recommendation allowed it to run, maintaining that the protesters had overreacted and were "blind to the irony" in Synge's masterpiece.[11]

The heavy consumption of liquor was sanctioned for centuries in Ireland. In Boston, the large number of Irish arrested for drunkenness contributed to the stereotype of the "Wild Hibernian," and police officials in the 1850s often noted that Irish-run saloons, concentrated on a street nicknamed Dublin Row, were altering the face of the city. To help overcome this problem, Father Theobald Mathew, the famous Irish temperance priest, toured Boston neighborhoods in the summer of 1849, stopping to administer the pledge to "batch after batch" of Irishmen and an occasional Negro or Indian. The *Pilot*, annoyed that the Irish had to get "beastly drunk" in order to have a good time, was able to report that within a few days after Father Mathew's visit, there was a significant drop in the number of arrests for drunkenness.[12]

John Boyle O'Reilly joined the campaign against inebriety and the saloon by advocating the construction of gymnasiums. A Charlestown parish bulletin attacked the Irish custom of "treating," whereby an individual's hospitality and generosity were measured by his willingness to buy drinks for his friends. Irish temperance societies lobbied against the sale of alcohol in public parks, liquor advertisements in Catholic newspapers, and the saloonkeepers' practice of flying Irish flags over their establishments on Saint Patrick's Day. They sponsored parish baseball teams and marching bands with flags reading "Keep Cool" and "Give me this water that I may not thirst." In 1909 a "Monster Field Day" drew more than 40,000 people to Franklin Park for games, dog shows, music, and juggling acts. Fifteen thousand youngsters took the pledge that day and carried home pictures of Father Mathew and messages warning against the evils of demon rum. The attempt by temperance advocates to discourage the Ancient Order of Hibernians from serving liquor at its meetings triggered the famous Sunday "beer socials" controversy in 1899. In a letter to a protemperance newspaper, one Irish reader reassured critics that the A.O.H. was not "going to the dogs" because of drinking and maintained that the fraternal organization owed its immense popularity to the fact that it did serve spirits at its functions. A.O.H. members in favor of "dry" meetings ultimately triumphed.[13]

In trying to combat the popularity of the saloon among the Irish, temperance societies were helpless against a social institution firmly rooted in the Irish past. The saloon fulfilled more than a customer's longing for a cold beer or a shot of whiskey. With its informal setting of wooden chairs, card tables, sawdust-covered floors, and portrait of John L. Sullivan or Mike "King" Kelly, the famous baseball player, it was a place where the Irish could congregate to discuss union issues or to exchange the latest news from the old country while enjoying a five-cent beer and a "free lunch" (mandated by law), consisting usually of bread, crackers, pickles, and meat stew. Ward boss politics flourished in this convivial atmosphere. Nomination papers could be circulated, and saloonkeepers, as officeholders, won votes from their customers on election day by offering them patronage jobs. When the "prince of jolliers," or the ward boss himself, made an appear-

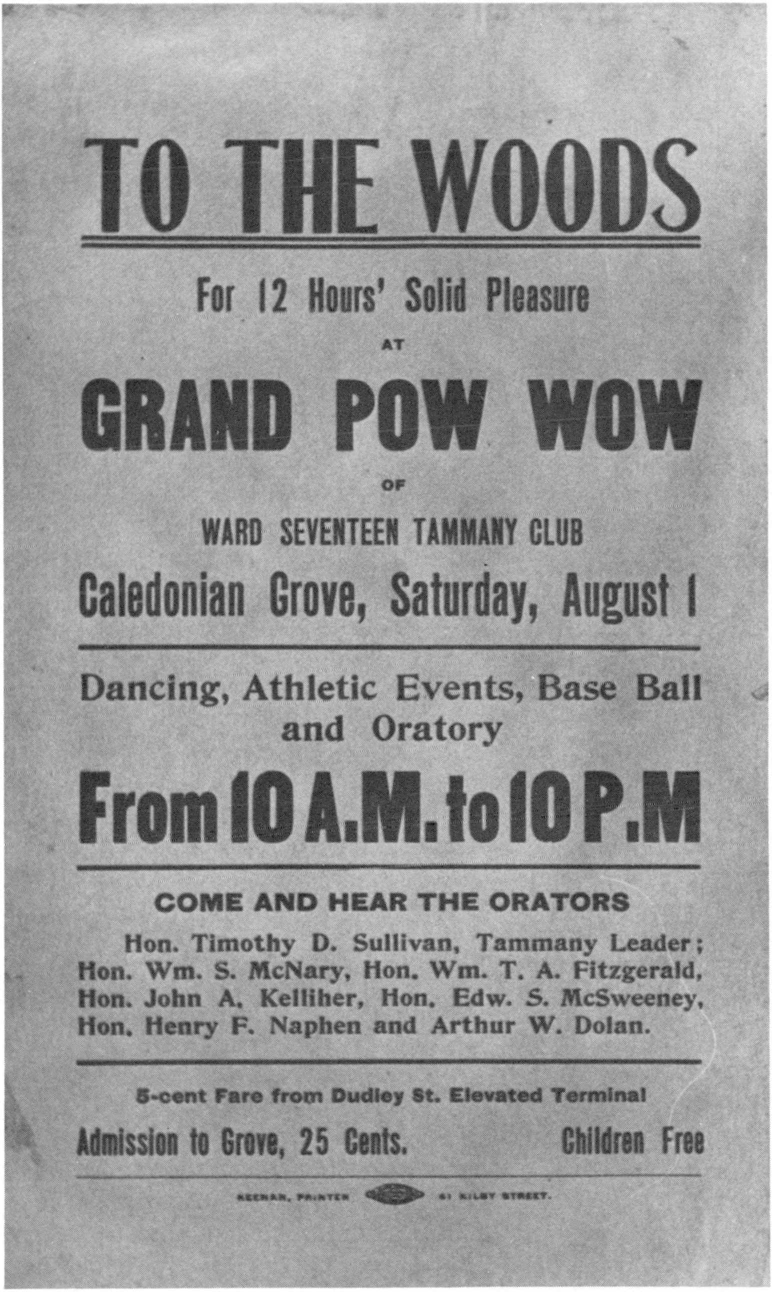

TO THE WOODS

For 12 Hours' Solid Pleasure

AT

GRAND POW WOW

OF

WARD SEVENTEEN TAMMANY CLUB

Caledonian Grove, Saturday, August 1

Dancing, Athletic Events, Base Ball and Oratory

From 10 A.M. to 10 P.M

COME AND HEAR THE ORATORS

Hon. Timothy D. Sullivan, Tammany Leader;
Hon. Wm. S. McNary, Hon. Wm. T. A. Fitzgerald,
Hon. John A. Kelliher, Hon. Edw. S. McSweeney,
Hon. Henry F. Naphen and Arthur W. Dolan.

5-cent Fare from Dudley St. Elevated Terminal

Admission to Grove, 25 Cents.   Children Free

KEENAN, PRINTER   61 KILBY STREET.

Fig. 19. Politics, as this early 1900s handbill makes clear, was as much a form of entertainment for the Boston Irish as it was a vehicle to discuss issues.

ance, he treated the house to a "free" round of drinks and lived up to his reputation as a storyteller by revealing the latest intrigues at City Hall and advising patrons where to place their money in a close election. (Although Irish politicians may have profited financially and professionally from their close affiliation with the liquor trade, they were frequently teetotalers—the only two things that ward boss Martin Lomasney overindulged in were applesauce and expensive underwear.)[14]

The average work week shortened steadily after 1890, and Irish politicians moved to exploit the desire of their nondrinking constitutents for recreation. Ward healers in Roxbury founded the Eustis Club in 1903 and furnished it with a reading room, billiard tables, and a cafeteria that was said to be a "model of neatness and comfort." James Michael Curley and his Tammany Club provided clothing, toys, and entertainment at Christmastime for needy children of Ward Seventeen and sponsored annual balls and picnics. The highlight of the summer season, picnics were announced by leaflets inviting young and old to come "To the Woods for 12 Hours' Solid Pleasure." Crowds as large as twenty thousand spent the day listening to speeches made by the "Big Chiefs" of the Democratic party and enjoying track and field events, baseball games, piano-smashing contests, "greased pig chases," and "old folks' dancing." Accounts of such picnics in the next morning's newspaper attested to the overwhelming success of the Irish politician as a provider of recreation and itemized the exact amounts of ham, hot dogs, rolls, ice cream, peanuts, and lemonade consumed by his constituents.[15]

The Irish enjoyed political speechmaking as another form of recreation. They had a rich oral tradition: Ireland's national heroes were master orators Robert Emmet, Henry Grattan, and Daniel O'Connell. As the *shanachie*, or village storyteller, began to disappear from the Irish countryside, the masses, who did not have a national theater, were left without a chief source of diversion. The nineteenth-century Irish politician, with his penchant for flamboyant rhetoric, vivid metaphors, witty anecdotes, and personal invective, inherited the responsibility of entertaining a people who came to value the way a public figure said something almost as much as what he said.[16]

Around election time the Boston Irish politician never overlooked an opportunity to provide "good theater" with his campaign antics and speechmaking. The excitement began at the moment nomination papers were filed. Candidates canvassed for key endorsements and accused each other of stooping to "dirty politics," such as employing hecklers or using sneezing powder to disrupt campaign meetings. The Irish, as heirs to Daniel O'Connell's legacy of mass participation in the democratic process, relished the exhilaration of the political rally. In 1910, thousands turned out with torches, placards, and banners to support mayoral candidate John F. Fitzgerald. Assisted by the newly invented automobile, "Honey Fitz" made a triumphant "whirlwind tour" of the city's twenty-five wards on election eve. When he crossed a bridge into the Irish district of South Boston, he was escorted out of his auto and into another drawn by a hundred "rope pullers" who towed the machine up the main avenue, just as in the old days admirers of O'Connell had hand-pulled his stagecoach through every Irish village.[17]

The candidate's speech was the climax of the campaign rally. Whether it was delivered by an accomplished orator such as Curley or Fitzgerald or by a "local spellbinder," an Irish political speech had certain distinct features. Like the new politicians of the Jacksonian era who were fond of contrasting their humble log cabin beginnings with those of their opponents, Boston's Irish politicians often compared their tenement house origins with those of Harvard-educated, Back Bay Brahmins. Just as politicians in Ireland had railed against John Bull, Curley and Fitzgerald, champions of the underdog, instinctively grasped the political usefulness of lampooning the English airs of the Brahmins. They could elicit a round of applause by claiming that, if elected, they would make the Brahmins pay their taxes like every other ordinary citizen. And a minute later they could evoke gales of laughter by maintaining that a patrician office seeker such as James Storrow could not recognize a pair of workingman's overalls if his life depended on it.[18]

Another outlet for the Irish was the world of "Society and

Clubdom." The Tipperary Men's Association brought the "exiled sons of Gallant Tipperary" together, and the Knights and Ladies of Saint Brendan helped to strengthen the bonds among those from County Kerry. A very conspicuous organization was the Ancient Order of Hibernians, whose origins could be traced to medieval Ireland. At first suspected by some American priests of being a revolutionary organization bent on provoking violence between management and labor, the A.O.H. could boast more than eight thousand members in Boston's Suffolk County by 1900. The order provided its brethren with inexpensive life insurance and ample opportunity to socialize, and its local divisions and chapters were named in honor of Irish heroes like Wolfe Tone and Brian Boru. A.O.H. parades, with marchers in full regalia and often carrying swords, were always a principal feature of Saint Patrick's Day celebrations.[19]

Two of the most prestigious social organizations were the Charitable Irish Society and the Catholic Union. Founded in 1737 to aid fellow immigrants, the Charitable Irish Society by the 1850s was primarily a wining and dining club for middle-class Irish. The Society held its annual Saint Patrick's Day dinner in Boston's most exclusive hotels, where prominent Yankees often were guests, and members took special pride in the fact that they represented the oldest Irish society in America. They marched with "blue-bloods" from the New England Historic Genealogical Society during the public ceremony in 1875 commemorating the hundredth anniversary of the Battle of Bunker Hill. The Catholic Union, dedicated to promoting Church interests in Boston, counted many Irishmen among its "élite" membership. The Union sponsored a lecture series on current topics, and its impressive South End clubhouse had a library, a billiard room, and a bowling alley where anyone accompanied by a female on Friday evenings was given preference among those waiting to try their luck at tenpins.[20]

The Irish, however, were routinely excluded from such Brahmin strongholds as the Somerset and Algonquin Clubs. Of 600 members belonging to the Somerset Club in 1917,

Fig. 20. Patrick J. Kennedy (second from left), a successful saloonkeeper, liquor dealer, politician, and grandfather of an American president, is shown here engaging in a card game with some friends.

only three, at the most, had Irish surnames. And at "The Country Club" in Brookline, where Yankee patricians played golf, tennis, polo, and curling and watched horse racing, the same discrimination prevailed. Without the prerequisite of membership in these clubs, few Irish were listed in the *Social Register*, the hallmark of full acceptance into Yankee Boston society. Social segregation carried over into summer resort areas around Boston. The Yankees tended to vacation in the North Shore towns of Nahant, Marblehead, and Beverly, while prominent Irish like O'Reilly, Donnelly, Gargan, and Fitzgerald summered in communities south of Boston and on Cape Cod.[21]

On March 17—Saint Patrick's Day—Irish throughout Boston celebrated the fact that they were Irish. Having dispelled the popular suspicion surrounding their allegiance to the Union by fighting in the Civil War, they asserted their new sense of belonging by turning their patron saint's feast day from a religious to a more secular event. Some chose to observe the day by attending temperance banquets, where toasts to Ireland were made with "sparkling water," while others celebrated at parish socials, music concerts, saloons, and theaters, which featured Irish plays for the entire month. The parade, which passed through downtown Boston and the neighborhoods of Charlestown, South Boston, and Dorchester, drew thousands of spectators, many of whom had decorated their residences and business establishments with portraits of Saint Patrick and banners proclaiming "Erin Go Bragh" ("Ireland Forever") and "Céad Míle Fáilte" ("A Hundred Thousand Welcomes").[22]

NOTES

1. *Boston Pilot*, 10 July and 19 June 1847; John F. Byrne, C.SS.R., *The Glories of Mary in Boston: A Memorial History of the Church of Our Lady of Perpetual Help (Mission Church), Roxbury, Mass. 1871–1921* (Boston: 1921), pp. 200, 416–53.

2. Oscar Handlin, *Boston's Immigrants, A Study in Acculturation*, rev. and enl. ed. (Cambridge, Mass.: 1959), p. 157; Robert Ernst, *Immigrant Life in New York City 1825–1863* (New York: 1949), pp. 127, 128; R. A. Burchell, *The San Francisco Irish, 1848–1880* (Berkeley, Calif.: 1980), p. 97; *Boston Pilot*, 17 February 1838, 5 November, 22 October 1853.

3. *Boston Pilot*, 1 and 8 October 1853, 17 February 1838, 22 and 15 October, 24 and 10 September 1853; Robert H. Lord, John E. Sexton, and Edward T. Harrington, *History of the Archdiocese of Boston*, 3 vols. (New York: 1944), 2:700, 701. The companies would, however, continue their activities under different names. Handlin, *Boston's Immigrants*, p. 157.

4. John J. Kane, "The Irish Wake: A Sociological Appraisal," *Sociological Symposium*, 1 (Fall 1968):10–15; Seán Ó Súilleabháin, *Irish Wake Amusements* (Cork: 1967), pp. 166–73; *Boston Pilot*, 18 August 1849.

5. John Rickards Betts, *America's Sporting Heritage, 1850–1950* (Reading, Mass.: 1974), pp. 162–64; *Donahoe's Magazine* 9 (May 1883):466, 467; ibid. 14 (November 1885):444–46; ibid. 20 (July–August 1888):24–31, 148–57.

6. *Boston Globe*, 9 July 1889; *British American Citizen*, 7 April 1888; *Boston Republic*, 19 July 1890; Betts, *America's Sporting Heritage*, p. 165; William V. Shannon, *The American Irish* (New York: rev. ed. 1966), pp. 95, 96.

7. Shannon, *American Irish*, pp. 97–102; Dale A. Somers, *The Rise of Sports in New Orleans, 1850–1900* (Baton Rouge, La.: 1972), pp. 159–73; *British American Citizen*, 7 April 1888; *Boston Globe*, 9 August 1887, 8 September 1892; John L. Sullivan, *Life and Reminiscences of a 19th Century Gladiator* (Boston: 1892), p. 176; *Boston Globe*, 8, 9, 26, 27 September 1892; Betts, *America's Sporting Heritage*, p. 166.

8. Thomas Ryan, *Recollections of an Old Musician* (New York: 1899), pp. 186–203; Handlin, *Boston's Immigrants*, p. 211; James Bernard Cullen, ed., *The Story of the Irish in Boston* (Boston: 1889), pp. 219–20; P. S. Gilmore, *History of the National Peace Jubilee and Great Musical Festival Held in the City of Boston, June, 1869* (Cambridge, Mass.: 1871), pp. 2, 17, 270, 275, 403, 526; *Boston Pilot*, 26 June 1869, 13 July 1872; Honor McCusker, *Fifty Years of Music in Boston* (Boston: 1938), pp. 23, 24; *Boston Republic*, 1 October 1892; William T. Campbell scrapbook, Music Department, Boston Public Library, pp. 68–70.

9. Dexter Smith, *Cyclopedia of Boston and Vicinity* (Boston: 1886), p. 238; Constance Rourke, *American Humor: A Study of the National Character* (New York: 1931), pp. 103, 138, 139, 141; Carl Wittke, "The Immigrant Theme on the American Stage," *Mississippi Valley Historical Review* 39 (September 1952):211–19; Carl Wittke, *The Irish in America* (Baton Rouge, La.: 1956), pp. 253–63; Earl F. Niehaus, *The Irish in New Orleans, 1800–1860* (Baton Rouge, La.: 1965), pp. 120–31; Sheila Tully, "Irish-American Reaction to John Millington Synge's *Playboy of the Western World*" (10 May 1978), p. 3, manuscript in the possession of Professor Andrew Buni, Department of History, Boston College, Newton, Mass. According to one actress in such nineteenth-century Boston "Irish pieces," theatergoers sometimes had to be turned away "in droves." (Brander Matthews and Lawrence Hutton, eds., *Actors and Actresses* 5, no. 5 [undated]:8, Harvard University Theatre Collection, Houghton Library, Cambridge, Mass.; *Boston Republic*, 26 March 1898, 27 September and 18 October 1890; Eugenia M. Coleman, "Dion Boucicault: His Contributions to the American Theatre" (Master's thesis, Boston College: 1965), pp. 45, 53; Roger Lane, "James Jeffrey Roche and the Boston Pilot," *New England Quarterly* 33 (September 1960):343. For advertisements for Irish plays see *Boston Daily Advertiser*, 19 March 1849, *Boston Herald*, 17 March 1871, and playbill in *Actors and Actresses*, "Wm. J. Florence," 5, no. 7 (1859).

10. Wittke, "Immigrant on Stage," pp. 220, 221, 227–30; *Boston Republic*, 2 and 23 January, 6 and 13 February, 27 August, 10 December 1892, 27 December 1890, 20 January 1900; Tully, "Irish-American Reaction to *Playboy*," pp. 3, 12, 15, 18, 29, 30–35; *The Complete Plays of John M. Synge* (New York: 1960), pp. 7–80, editor unknown.

11. Tully, "Irish-American Reaction to *Playboy*," pp. 1–5, 25; *Boston Globe*, 17 October 1911; *Boston Pilot*, 21 October 1911; newspaper clippings, 16, 17, 18 October 1911 in John F. Fitzgerald scrapbooks (hereafter cited as F.N.C.), Holy Cross College Archives.

12. Richard Stivers, *A Hair of the Dog: Irish Drinking and American Stereotype* (University Park, Pa.: 1976), pp. 15–33, 81–88, 98–100; Handlin, *Boston's Immigrants*, p. 121; Stanley K. Schultz, *The Culture Factory: Boston Public Schools, 1789–1860* (New York: 1973), p. 239; Lord, Sexton, and Harrington, *History of the Archdiocese*, 2:643–47; *Boston Evening Transcript*, 24 July 1849; *Boston Pilot*, 4 August, 28 July 1849.

13. John R. Betts, "John Boyle O'Reilly and the American Paideia," *Éire-Ireland* 2 (1967):48, 49; Joan Bland, S.N.D., *Hibernian Crusade: The Story of the Catholic Total Abstinence Union of America* (Washington, D.C.: 1951), pp. 48, 138, 224, 258; *Sacred Heart Review*, 2 December 1899; Stivers, *Hair of the Dog*, pp. 31, 86, 87; Maurice Dinneen, *The Catholic Total Abstinence Movement in the Archdiocese of Boston* (Boston:

1908), pp. 102–10; *Boston Pilot*, 22 March 1851; *Boston Post*, 27 July 1909; *Sacred Heart Review*, 2 September, 30 December 1899, 6 and 20 January, 3 February, 2 June 1900.

14. Stivers, *Hair of the Dog*, p. 121–25; Marjorie R. Fallows, *Irish Americans: Identity and Assimilation* (Englewood Cliffs, N.J.: 1979), pp. 50, 51; Jay P. Dolan, *Catholic Revivalism: The American Experience, 1830–1900* (South Bend, Ind.: 1978), p. 152; Herbert Marshall Zolot, *The Issue of Good Government and James Michael Curley: Curley and the Boston Scene from 1897–1918* (Ann Arbor, Mich.: University Microfilms International, 1975), pp. 152–55; Jon M. Kingsdale, "The 'Poor Man's Club': Social Functions of the Urban Working-Class Saloon," *American Quarterly* 25 (October 1973) :472–85; William I. Cole and Kellogg Durland, "Substitutes for the Saloon in Boston," in *Substitutes for the Saloon*, ed. Raymond Calkins (Boston: 1901), pp. 321–23, 330; Edward M. Levine, *The Irish and Irish Politicians* (South Bend, Ind.: 1966), pp. 116–19; James Michael Curley, *I'd Do It Again: A Record of All My Uproarious Years* (Englewood Cliffs, N.J.: 1957), pp. 27, 45; Robert A. Woods, ed., *The City Wilderness* (New York: 1898; reprint edition, 1970), pp. 123, 128, 129, 137, 138; Leslie G. Ainley, *Boston Mahatma* (Boston: 1949), pp. 8, 9.

15. Stephen Hall Hardy, *Organized Sport and the Search for Community: Boston, 1865–1915* (Ann Arbor, Mich: University Microfilms International, 1980), pp. 80, 81; Curley, *I'd Do It Again*, pp. 18, 53–55, 62, 64; newspaper clippings in James Michael Curley scrapbook dated 1903, Holy Cross College Archives (hereafter cited as C.N.C.); *Boston Sunday Globe*, 30 July 1905, 26 August 1906; *Boston Post*, 30 July 1908.

16. Andrew E. Malone, *The Irish Drama* (reissued, New York: 1965), pp. 2–8; Zolot, *The Issue of Good Government*, pp. 229, 230. A major figure in Boston politics for nearly fifty years, James Michael Curley considered his oratorical ability to be his primary asset in helping him to win elections. William Jay Foley, "Public Speaking in the Political Career of James M. Curley" (Ph.D. diss., University of Wisconsin, 1952), p. iii.

17. Ainley, *Boston Mahatma*, pp. 53–59; newspaper clipping dated 1913, and others dated 4, 6, and 10 January 1914, 1, 7, 10, 11 January 1910, F.N.C.; Lawrence J. McCaffrey, *Daniel O'Connell and the Repeal Year* (Lexington, Ky.: 1966), pp. 51–56; Frederick A. Bushee, "The Invading Host," in *Americans in Process*, ed. Robert A. Woods (Boston: 1902), p. 63.

18. Newspaper clippings, 1 and 2 January 1910, F.N.C.; Dennis Clark, *The Irish in Philadelphia, Ten Generations of Urban Experience* (Philadelphia: 1973), pp. 124, 125; Joseph F. Dinneen, *The Purple Shamrock: The Hon. James Michael Curley of Boston* (New York: 1949), pp. 40, 41; John Henry Cutler, *"Honey Fitz": Three Steps to the White House—The Life and Times of John F. (Honey Fitz) Fitzgerald* (Indianapolis, Ind.: 1962), pp. 32–34, 41, 42; Zolot, *The Issue of Good Government*, pp. 230–32; newspaper clippings and leaflets, 1 and 2 January 1910, F.N.C. For other examples of Brahmin baiting see Cutler, *"Honey Fitz,"* pp. 129, 130, 136; newspaper clipping dated January 1914, F.N.C.; and *Boston Herald*, 30 November 1909.

19. Cutler, *"Honey Fitz,"* p. 80; *Constitution and By-Laws of the Tipperary Men's Association of Boston* (Boston: 2 August 1908), p. 4, located in the Stephen O'Meara Papers, deposited at the Boston Public Library; *Boston Republic*, 18 May 1907, 12 May 1900; Wittke, *The Irish in America*, pp. 196, 197; *Memoirs, Boston Diocese*, vol. 4, 3 and

20 January 1859, deposited at the Archdiocese of Boston Archives, Brighton, Mass.; *Boston Pilot*, 5 May 1900, including *Ancient Order of Hibernians' Supplement*.

20. Handlin, *Boston's Immigrants*, pp. 155, 160; Charles T. Burke, *The Silver Key: A History of the Charitable Irish Society Founded in Boston 1737* (Boston?: 1973), pages unnumbered; Lord, Sexton, and Harrington, *History of the Archdiocese*, 3:388–90; *The Catholic Union of Boston Charter, Constitution* (30 November 1896), p. 24, Thomas F. Ring Papers, deposited at the Boston office of the Society of Saint Vincent de Paul.

21. *A Brief History of the Somerset Club of Boston, With a List of Past and Present Members, 1852–1913*, prepared by A Committee of the Club (Boston: 1914), pp. 35–68, deposited at the Boston Public Library; *Constitution of the Somerset Club With a List of Its Officers and Members June, 1917* (Boston: 1917), pp. 53–72; Frederic H. Curtiss and John Heard, *The Country Club 1882–1932* (Brookline, Mass.: 1932), pp. 9, 56, 57, 65, 119, 120, 139, 140, 169–74, deposited at the Boston Public Library; Arthur W. Brayley, *The Clubs of Boston* (Boston: 1891), pp. 17–29, 227–32A, *Social Register Association, Social Register, Boston, 1914*, 28, no. 5 (New York: 1913), pp. 5–180. On the subject of club membership, Charles H. Taylor wrote to Stephen O'Meara, a distinguished Boston Irish journalist, in 1898, "We fellows who are making our own way in life cannot join the Somerset, and would freeze if we did." (Taylor to O'Meara, 20 October 1898, O'Meara Papers.) For Yankee domination of cultural and literary institutions such as the Boston Athenaeum, the Lowell Institute, and the Massachusetts Historical and Horticultural Societies, see Ronald Story, *The Forging of an Aristocracy: Harvard & the Boston Upper Class, 1800–1870* (Middletown, Conn.: 1980); *The North Shore Blue Book and Social Register, 1917* (Boston: 1917), pp. 12–19, 33 50, 59–69, 152–87; Joseph E. Garland, *Boston's North Shore: Being An Account of Life Among the Noteworthy, Fashionable, Wealthy, Eccentric and Ordinary 1823–1890* (Boston: 1978), pp. 95–100, 181, 233–53; Francis G. McManamin, *The American Years of John Boyle O'Reilly, 1870–1890* (New York: 1976), p. 291; Katherine E. Conway and Mabel Ward Cameron, *Charles Francis Donnelly, A Memoir* (New York: 1909), p. 251; Joseph Smith, *Thomas J. Gargan, A Memorial* (Boston: 1910), p. 63; newspaper clipping, 24 July 1913, F.N.C.; *South Shore Blue Book and Social Register* (Arlington, Mass.: 1922), pp. 174–208; *Boston Republic*, 26 July 1890, 20 July 1907.

22. *Boston Herald*, 16 and 18 March 1871, 18 March 1872, 17 March 1873; *Boston Republic*, 12 March 1892; Wittke, *The Irish in America*, pp. 198–201. Some 1,000 people from the Boston vicinity turned out for Orangemen's Day festivities in July 1893, when one speaker contended that William of Orange's defeat of Catholic King James II at the Battle of the Boyne in 1690 was "a victory of light over darkness, and of truth over wrong." *British American Citizen*, 22 July 1893.

6
The Irish and the Melting Pot

There are no classes or races, but one human
brotherhood;
There are no creeds to be outlawed, no colors of
skin debarred;
Mankind is one in its rights and wrongs—one
right, one hope, one guard.

John Boyle O'Reilly, 1884

The greatest threat to any struggling minority group is
another struggling minority group. The Irish competed for
employment, housing, education, and political recognition
with Boston's free Negro population during the 1840s and
later with Jews, Italians, and other ethnic groups. Crowded
into a rundown section known as "Nigger Hill," Boston's
blacks numbered around 2,000 in 1850. Irish and blacks
fighting for jobs as longshoremen and warehousemen became
archenemies. Negroes joined Yankees in condemning the Irish
for being priest-ridden, paupers, drunkards, and rioters, and
in an effort to protect what little property they owned on Elm
Street, some of them signed a petition in the 1850s to keep the
Irish from encroaching on their neighborhood.[1]
    Talk of abolition increased the antagonism. Opposed in
principle to slavery, the Irish laborer recoiled at the idea of
having to compete with four million freedmen for employment. The Irish also distrusted the motives of the abolitionists, or "Nigger-worshippers," as the *Pilot* called them, who
were known to be anti-Catholic and anti-immigrant. While

abolitionists championed the rights of slaves hundreds of miles away in Dixie, they maintained a sphinxlike silence regarding the New England factory system that exploited the Irish worker. The *Pilot* asked how black sympathizers like Harriet Beecher Stowe could address antislavery societies in England and remain unmoved by the anguish and suffering across the Irish Sea. In a country that favored whites over blacks, the Boston Irish found themselves in a community that preferred Negroes to Catholic immigrants.[2]

In 1854, the city's abolitionists threatened to attack authorities in order to prevent the return of a fugitive slave to his Southern master, and the *Pilot* condemned them as lawbreakers. When the Boston public schools were officially integrated in 1855, the Irish were less than enthusiastic about their children sharing classrooms with Negroes and were particularly critical of wealthy Yankees, abolitionists included, who enrolled their offspring in private schools or the highly select Boston Latin School. The *Pilot* posed the question whether black children possessed the mental ability to compete successfully with white students. And when John Brown tried to capture the Harpers Ferry arsenal in October in 1859, the *Pilot* was glad to report that not one Irishman was implicated in the raid. The only Irishmen at the scene of the attack, the newspaper boasted, were marines like Sergeant Quinn, who lost his life trying to recapture the arsenal. At a ceremony in Boston to honor Brown, a mob, which included some Irishmen, stormed the stage, forcing Frederick Douglass, the black abolitionist, to retreat down a flight of stairs, but only after he had defended himself as if he were "a trained pugilist."[3]

As long as the Civil War was waged to preserve the Union rather than to free the slaves, the Irish supported the Northern cause. But when President Lincoln started talking about emancipating the slaves, the *Pilot* declared that the slaves themselves would reject the President's proposal because "they love their masters, as dogs do, and servile plantation life is the life nature intended for them." In 1863, when the Army of the Potomac contemplated forming all-Negro fighting units, the *Pilot* remarked that the body odor emanating from twenty thousand marching black soldiers would be a dead giveaway to Confederates ten miles away.[4]

The Irish also opposed a federal conscription law passed shortly after the Emancipation Proclamation in 1863. Unlike many avid abolitionists who could commute their military service by paying $300 for a substitute, poor working-class Irish and native-born Americans were prime candidates to fill the depleted army ranks. The Irish were infuriated at the blatant inequities of the law and reacted violently. In New York City, for example, three days of rioting against the draft in July of 1863 left more than seventy people dead. In Boston, some Irish priests, themselves liable to conscription, incited their parishioners: at one North End parish, an antidraft meeting broke up noisily with "cheers" for Jefferson Davis. Mobs assaulted Negroes and ransacked stores along State Street in an effort to procure firearms to resist federal marshals issuing draft notices. Protecting an armory from these "Mobocrats," as William Lloyd Garrison called them, the state militia finally fired on the crowd, killing six people, four of them Irish.[5]

After the surrender at Appomattox and John Boyle O'Reilly's appointment as *Pilot* editor in 1876, relations between Irish and blacks improved. In 1887, for instance, to honor Irishman Patrick Carr and a black named Crispus Attucks, who fell at the Boston Massacre in 1770, the two groups worked closely to overcome strong opposition to a monument on the Boston Common which would commemorate those whom some Brahmins considered "hoodlums, rioters, and ruffians." Unlike most Irishmen, O'Reilly had some previous exposure to nonwhites before arriving in Boston in 1870. In an Australian penal colony, the ex-Fenian had come to admire the aborigines, particularly for their love of music and nature. As *Pilot* editor, he gave substantial coverage to Negro social and cultural activities, praised the appointment of blacks to public office, and even condoned racial intermarriage.[6]

During the early years of Reconstruction, O'Reilly advised Negroes to seek advancement gradually and to obtain an education before demanding social and political equality. But the South's harsh treatment of the freedmen forced him to greater

Fig. 21. John Boyle O'Reilly (1844–1890), poet, editor, and champion of racial and social justice.

militancy. As he passed through Nashville in 1885, the squalid living conditions and segregation in hotels and other public places convinced him "that something was the matter either with God or humanity in the South." Negroes were subjected to shootings, hangings, and floggings, and O'Reilly saw little reason to expect that the perpetrators of such crimes would ever be convicted by their peers. After the murder of some Negroes in Mississippi in 1886, he advised blacks to mobilize politically. "If I were a colored man," he asserted, "I should use political parties, as I would a club or a hatchet, to smash the prejudice that dared to exclude my children from a public school, or myself from a public hall, theater, or hotel." When an Alabama senator suggested that the best way to alleviate racial tension was to deport all Negroes back to Africa, O'Reilly retorted that such a scheme "could find lodgement only in the brain of a belated fossil."[7]

He criticized eight white students in Indianapolis who protested against sharing a graduation platform with a black classmate, and he condemned New York policemen who threatened to strike rather than allow a Negro to join the force. Upon denouncing the Franklin Typographical Society of Boston for refusing membership to a Negro printer, he was charged, by a reader who canceled his *Pilot* subscription, with attempting to mongrelize the white race. O'Reilly responded: "We are sorry that such sentiments should come from one who boasts of belonging to 'the faithful Irish.'" He added: "There is nothing Irish about his principles; and we are glad to receive the 'stop my *Pilot*' of such a man." In 1890, when Clement Garnett Morgan, a Negro, was the commencement day class orator at Harvard College, O'Reilly made it the occasion for another attack on Northern racial hypocrisy. "When his oration was ended," he wrote, "and Morgan stepped out of Harvard and into the world, he ceased to be a 'gentleman' and an equal, and at one descent fell to the level of 'the nigger,' who could never be invited to one's house or proposed at one's club, who would be refused a room at nearly all leading hotels, even in the North, and who would not be tolerated even in church in the half-empty pew of polite worshipers."[8]

O'Reilly's sudden death in August of 1890 stunned Boston's Negro community. For a full day, black and white mourners paid their last respects before the bier in Charlestown's Saint Mary's Church. And on the coffin lid, just above the shamrocks on O'Reilly's chest, blacks had affectionately placed palm branches. They had lost their greatest friend in Boston since Wendell Phillips.[9]

Within a Church that was overwhelmingly Irish, there were about one thousand black Catholics in 1900. One well-known convert to Catholicism, Robert Morris, became the first black to be admitted to the Boston bar, and until his death in 1882, he enjoyed a highly successful law practice made up mostly of Irish clients. At his parish church, he spotted an eager, bright-eyed altar boy named Patrick Andrew Collins and gave the future congressman and mayor a job as an office boy. A black priest, Father James Healy, was indispensable to John Bernard Fitzpatrick, the Bishop of Boston from 1846 to 1866. Suffering from poor health, he relied on the talented, aristocratic-looking Healy for advice and assistance in administering

Fig. 22. At parishes such as Saint Mary's in the North End, black Catholics worshiped alongside their Irish coreligionists.

his sprawling archdiocese. In 1866, Healy, in return for his dedication, was appointed pastor of the newly built church of Saint James, where his color was a subject of great discussion among the predominantly Irish congregation. Addressed as "Father James" by his flock, the black priest, however, felt perfectly at home. Privately, he said that he had learned his lessons on how to "tame" and "rule" an Irish parish from his mentor, Fitzpatrick.[10]

The Catholic Church in Boston took measures to meet the needs of its black brethren. Catholic charitable institutions, supported by Irish contributions, accepted Negro orphans, and in 1889 the Society of Saint Vincent de Paul established a parish conference, named in honor of Peter Claver, a Negro saint, to deal with black poverty. In 1898, Negroes attending a South End Irish parish sought permission to hold separate religious services and were allowed to do so in the basement.

Ten years later black Catholics were given their own church, a dilapidated building abandoned by Irish parishioners who had migrated to more desirable parts of the city. The church's name: Saint Patrick's.[11]

Although they were few in number and traditionally tied to the party of Lincoln, Negro voters were wooed by Irish American politicians such as Mayors John F. Fitzgerald and James Michael Curley. Campaigning just before the 1907 election, Fitzgerald addressed a black audience meeting at Faneuil Hall to protest President Theodore Roosevelt's dismissal one year earlier of an entire Negro battalion from the United States Army for their alleged involvement in the Brownsville, Texas riot. He was cheered wildly upon condemning the President's actions as being discriminatory. Fitzgerald remained acutely sensitive to black aspirations and was praised by Boston's leading Negro newspaper, the *Guardian*, as a man "free from all color prejudice." In 1910 he appointed a black attorney to head the city's Weights and Measures Department, and when some of the department's personnel protested their new boss, he accused them of prejudice and ordered them to resign. At other times, the mayor used his influence to avoid racial conflict generated by the showing of plays derogatory to blacks, such as *The Clansman*.[12]

James Michael Curley, who succeeded Fitzgerald as mayor, was less successful in relating to blacks. He appointed some Negroes to high municipal posts, named a city street in honor of Frederick Douglass, and championed the right of a black soldier to be interred in Arlington National Cemetery. But, as mayor, he alienated thousands of Negroes by refusing to prevent *The Birth of a Nation*, D. W. Griffith's white supremacist film, from being shown in Boston in 1915. William Monroe Trotter, the *Guardian* editor, implored Curley to block the film, then resorted to legal methods and was unsuccessful in both—the judge refused to ban it. Trotter persisted, lacing into Curley at a Faneuil Hall rally. "Where is the valiant Jim Curley of old, the friend of the people . . . lovable Jim Curley, whom we colored people supported for the mayoralty against the advice of some of our white friends? If this was an attack on the Irish race," Trotter concluded, "he would find a way pretty quick to stop it."[13]

Fleeing from czarist oppression, more than 64,000 Russian and Eastern European Jews found their way to Boston between 1875 and 1910. Irishmen in Donegal Square watched these strangers moving into their already congested North End neighborhood, with their unintelligible speech, strange eating habits, peculiar dress, long beards, and allegedly socialistic ideas. The two groups clashed on several issues. The Jewish newcomers, in a city taxed by a chronic housing shortage, caused rents to skyrocket. And when working-class Irish families in the North End were forced to move or were evicted, they attributed their misfortunes to the intruders. Then there were the hard feelings caused by the "Jewish passion for the unearned increment," or real estate speculation, and Francis Casey, a North End Jesuit priest, noted anxiously that Jewish landlords were "encroaching upon our domain" in the North End. Limited recreational facilities also produced conflict. During the hot summer of 1911, Jews sought relief at South Boston beaches traditionally used by the Irish, who became incensed at this invasion by Italians and Lithuanians as well as Jews. Irish policemen in the early 1900s harassed Jewish peddlers and grocers, charging them with violation of the blue laws, and disrupted their weddings on the pretext that union-paid musicians violated city ordinances prohibiting work on Sunday.[14]

The Jewish community also resented Irish efforts to dictate policy within the Boston public schools. When, for instance, the Irish successfully lobbied for courses in Irish history as a part of the grammar school curriculum, the *Advocate*, a Jewish newspaper, asserted that such studies were useful only to those contemplating careers as ward bosses. Attempts to introduce Gaelic into the schools prompted the *Advocate* to complain, "When will it end?" Jewish public school students had to listen to Catholic and Protestant classmates singing carols at Christmastime. Contending that such songs were contr their religious beliefs, Jewish leaders in 1916 filed a cor with authorities. John Sullivan, Boston's chief legal c dismissed it, claiming that carols were intended primarily as a form of "vocal exercise" rather than as a religious ceremony. In a school system staffed by Irish administrators, the *Advocate* claimed that "pull, favoritism, and chance" determined whether one was hired or promoted, and it charged two school officials with discriminatory hiring practices. One was the principal of a school with a predominantly Jewish student body and a forty-five-member faculty which contained not a single Jew.[15]

The Irish and the Jews were not always at odds. In 1891, when some Jewish immigrants were detained for suspected illegal immigration, Owen A. Galvin, a prominent Irish American attorney, helped obtain their release, and when the Boston City Hospital refused to admit Jewish patients because they were aliens, the Carney Hospital accepted them without hesitation. Jews, in turn, assisted at fund-raising affairs conducted by the sisters at the Carney and publicly praised the Irish as a high-minded and "indomitable race." The Jews and the Irish were able to break bread together politically for two reasons. First, because Jews tended to enter the professions and the business world, they were never regarded as a threat to Irish control over the Democratic party and related blue-collar patronage jobs. Second, the Irish, removed only a generation or two from the Great Hunger and the Crossing, grudgingly respected and admired a people who, like themselves, suffered for their religious convictions and way of life. The practical-minded Irish politician, in catering to the Jewish vote, could appear just as content eating kosher food as he did eating corned beef and cabbage and could appear as solemn in a synagogue wearing a *yarmulke* as he did in a Catholic church with his head uncovered. He never took the small Jewish vote for granted; it could be decisive in a close campaign between warring factions of the city's Irish Democratic party. Some Jewish leaders used the power associated with ethnic bloc voting to gain recognition and concessions from the shrewd politicians, Curley, Fitzgerald, and Martin Lomasney.[16]

To the thousands of Jews residing in his political domain,

Ward Eight, State Representative Lomasney was something of a messiah and something of a despot. He could be found almost any day at his headquarters, called the Hendricks Club, dispensing jobs, money, and political favors to his immigrant constituency. Late each day, he would go on a six-mile tour of his district, always carrying an umbrella and preferring to walk on the shady side of the street, because as a boy he had witnessed the death of his father from heat stroke. He would stop to listen to Jewish pushcart dealers' complaints with the licensing boards and to landlords' requests for favors from the city building inspector. One Mr. Finkelstein tried to break Lomasney's stranglehold on the election of representatives for the West End by running for office. Making a strong showing in the primary, Finkelstein boasted to Lomasney that in the general election Lomasney would have no alternative but to support him. Lomasney informed the young upstart that he would defeat him with an ordinary newspaper boy. As predicted, Finkelstein lost out to Louis Orenberg, a fellow Jew and Lomasney's hand-picked newsboy.[17]

Like Lomasney, Mayor Fitzgerald had a good rapport with Boston's Jews. Because of the large number of Jewish children in the public schools, Fitzgerald appreciated the Jewish community's desire to have one of its own on the Boston School Committee. And, despite Yankee charges that he was giving official sanction to a quota system, he persisted in asserting that one of the five positions on the School Committee should go to a Jew and helped one win election to the Committee in 1913. The majority of Jewish voters supported James Michael Curley in his first successful mayoralty campaign, in gratitude for his strenuous opposition to immigration restriction while serving in Congress. Curley ingratiated himself with his Jewish supporters by speaking at gatherings of the Young Men's Hebrew Association and at rallies opposing immigration restriction and by posing for official photographs with a Boston Jewish delegation bound for Atlanta, Georgia in 1915 to protest the murder trial of Leo M. Frank, a Jew unjustly convicted of murdering a thirteen-year-old gentile girl who worked in the pencil factory he managed. At the 1916 national convention of B'nai B'rith held in Boston, the mayor received thunderous applause when describing Louis Brandeis, a recent appointee to the Supreme Court, as "as able an American as has ever breathed the breath of life." (It was significant that Brandeis's appointment had been strongly opposed by Boston's Yankee legal establishment.) When a city planning board blamed the deterioration of housing in East Boston on Jewish families living there, Curley condemned the report as a "flagrant insult" to them. Poor housing was attributable to lack of income, not to nationality, he asserted, and ordered city printers to delete the derogatory remarks from the official report.[18]

The 49,000 Italians from Sicily and southern Italy who arrived in East Boston between 1875 and 1910 had little time to appreciate their newly won freedom from virtual serfdom. As they moved into the North End, they first had to defend themselves against some of their Irish neighbors. Parents complained of having to accompany their children to school in order to protect them from Irish classmates, and Italian fishermen pulling into port along the Boston waterfront after dark often chose to remain on board until morning rather than risk being assaulted by roving Irish street gangs. When Sicilians began wielding the stiletto, these attacks diminished, but, as Father Casey noted in 1895, there were still instances of fistfights between these groups. Commenting on the large crowd that had congregated near his rectory in the North End to watch an Irish lad beat up an Italian opponent, the priest noted in his diary that he "could not attract so many to a sermon."[19]

Uncomfortable in an English-speaking Church controlled mostly by Irish Catholic priests, Boston's Italians also disagreed with the hierarchy on the administration and financial support of local parishes. Accustomed to having a greater voice in parish affairs, they were far less predisposed than Irish churchgoers to accept without question the dictates of the pastor or priest. In Italy the state was principally responsible for the financial upkeep of the Church; in Boston the priest looked directly to his parishioners for contributions. Asked to donate to the offertory basket and to pay fees for baptisms, marriages, and funerals in order to defray parish expenses, it was not surprising that the Italians viewed the Irish pastor as being "money-mad." In the old country, regular church attendance was expected only of females; Italian men in Boston discovered that no Catholic was exempt from this obligation. Some Irishmen concluded that the Italian immigrants were anticlerical—Catholic in name only.[20]

Different modes of religious expression prompted further alienation. Italian church services were far more demonstrative than those of the more decorous Irish. No Irishman, for instance, would enter a church wearing a hat and puffing on a cigar; nor would he profess his human frailties prostrating himself before a crucifix or Station of the Cross. The Irish priest, whose devotions centered around the all-male Holy Trinity, encountered the matriarchal Italian family, which focused on the Madonna and Child. When the Church of the Sacred Heart of Jesus and Saint Leonard of Port Maurice became Italian parishes, the tensions of mixed congregations lessened. No longer subjected to sermons on the problems of Ireland and the Land League, Italian churchgoers could light as many candles as they wished to their favorite village saints, listen to hymns sung in the memory-filled, cantilene fashion of the old country, and, most of all, be consoled in their hours of need by a priest bearing an Italian name.[21]

On occasion, however, Italians were forced to seek assistance from the Irish, who tended to be better off financially. In 1911, the Italians received aid from the Catholic Immigration Bureau, which had the strong endorsement of Cardinal O'Connell. In addition to providing various religious and social services, the Bureau sponsored a cadet corps in hopes of disciplining Italian youths and bringing them closer to the Church. But there was a limit to diocesan funds, and Cardinal O'Connell lost patience with the Italians after repeated requests for aid. When the League of Catholic Women asked for money to expand services in the North End in 1915, O'Connell responded that it was "high time that the Italians should do something to help themselves."[22]

In an effort to maintain the dignified image of his Church,

O'Connell tried to moderate the Italians' feast days in honor of village saints. To non-Italians the festivals hardly resembled religious ceremonies. Italian men carried on their shoulders a statue of their favorite saint, accompanied by bands, fireworks, and barefoot women carrying candles. As the procession wound its way through North End streets, residents leaned out of tenement house windows and attached money to the statue. O'Connell discouraged these festivals and usually permitted them only upon assurance by Italian pastors that "due religious decorum" would be maintained.[23]

Concentrated in the building and construction trades, Italians were pitted against the Irish by employers who used them as strikebreakers. In 1876, the *Pilot* criticized foremen at a construction site for hiring "Italian serfs" to replace Irish laborers who had struck for better wages and working conditions. A quarter of a century later, Italians had to be protected from rock-throwing strikers by heavy police escort while being imported to replace Boston freight handlers who had walked off the job during a labor dispute. Many Italians allowed themselves to be used as pawns in order to accumulate enough savings to return to the old country. They had experienced discrimination in Cardinal O'Connell's church and could hardly expect equitable treatment in labor organizations monopolized by Irish officials. Consequently, they saw little advantage in spending their hard-earned money on union dues. Many were easy prey to the notorious *padrones*, who exacted exorbitant fees for acting as middlemen between their fellow Italians and employers—a practice that threatened to undermine the higher standard of living enjoyed by union members.[24]

In 1904 the Italians established their own Laborers' Union with some 1,600 members. At first reluctant to associate with the Boston Central Labor Union, an Irish-led organization that was a local affiliate of the American Federation of Labor, they soon petitioned the Central Union for an A.F.L. charter, which was granted after some difficulty. Working in alliance with Irish labor organizers and politicians, the Italians later benefited from agreements which gave preference to union members on city-funded construction projects.[25]

Only 11 percent of Boston's Italians were eligible to vote in 1910, and they usually voted Republican because they distrusted the Democratic Irish politician or because they associated the word "Republican" with Garibaldian idealism. Others turned to the G.O.P. in the belief that its position on a high protective tariff saved their jobs as factory workers. Mayor Fitzgerald, however, used his newspaper, the *Republic*, to praise Italians for continuing such customs as feast day celebrations. Despite his good intentions, Curley was hissed at by Italians at a 1915 public hearing called to protest the inadequate enforcement of sanitation and building codes by city officials in the North End. His tendency and that of various Irish societies to turn the observance of Christopher Columbus Day into an Irish affair also infuriated nationalistic elements of the Italian community.[26]

By functioning as an intermediary between Yankee Boston and the newer immigrants, the Irish were largely responsible for determining whether America's melting pot would melt or shatter. Products of a European past that made them suspicious of government, the newer immigrants learned from Irish ward bosses that in Boston a vote meant something and that by joining hands with the Curleys and the Lomasneys they could achieve better public services. From Irish trade union leaders, unskilled foreign laborers learned how to organize collectively in order to combat an economic system that too often brutalized them individually. All Catholic immigrants who cherished their faith were indebted to Irish priests, who struggled to ensure that the Catholic Church—universal, authoritarian, and adaptive—would survive and flourish in the Protestant city of Reverend Phillips Brooks and King's Chapel.

Troubled by increasing national violence between management and immigrant labor in the late 1890s, scholars at Harvard and other leading universities formed immigrant restriction leagues and, alarmed by the radical changes in America's racial composition, resorted to publishing pseudoscientific tracts that postulated the superiority of the Nordic race over southern and eastern Europeans. Confident that the republic could survive as a pluralistic society, the Boston Irish, in union halls, smoke-filled ward rooms, and ethnically diverse parishes across the city, demonstrated—if somewhat imperfectly—how right they really were.[27]

NOTES

1. John Daniels, *In Freedom's Birthplace: A Study of the Boston Negroes* (Boston: 1914), Table I, p. 457; Leon F. Litwack, *North of Slavery: The Negro in the Free States, 1790–1860* (Chicago, Ill.: 1961), pp. 155–65; Oscar Handlin, *Boston's Immigrants, A Study in Acculturation*, rev. and enl. ed. (Cambridge, Mass.: 1959), pp. 69, 70, 96, 205, 357, n. 104.

2. Handlin, *Boston's Immigrants*, pp. 132, 133; Francis Robert Walsh, *The Boston Pilot: A Newspaper for the Irish Immigrant, 1829–1908* (Ann Arbor, Mich.: University Microfilms International, 1969), pp. 120, 121, 127; *Boston Pilot*, 25 July 1863.

3. Walsh, *A Newspaper for the Irish Immigrant*, pp. 135, 136, 141, 142, 146; Stanley K. Schultz, *The Culture Factory: Boston Public Schools, 1789–1860* (New York: 1973), pp. 193, 194, 205, 206; *Boston Pilot*, 6 October 1855, 10 December 1859; James Oliver Horton and Lois E. Horton, *Black Bostonians: Family Life and Community Struggle in the Antebellum North* (New York: 1979), p. 125.

4. *Boston Pilot*, 14 December 1861, 22 February and 4 October 1862; Donald Martin Jacobs, "A History of the Boston Negro from the Revolution to the Civil War" (Ph.D. diss., Boston University, 1968), p. 366.

5. J. G. Randall and David Donald, *The Civil War and Reconstruction* (Lexington, Mass., second ed., revised: 1969), pp. 313, 314, 316, 317; William V. Shannon, *The American Irish* (New York: rev. ed., 1966), pp. 56–58; Robert H. Lord, John E. Sexton, and Edward T. Harrington, *History of the Archdiocese of Boston*, 3 vols. (New York: 1944), 2:708; *Memoirs, Boston Diocese*, vol. 5, 14 July 1863, Archdiocese of Boston Archives, Brighton, Mass. (hereafter cited as A.B.A.); Michael Hindus, "A City of Mobocrats and Tyrants: Mob Violence in Boston, 1747–1863," *Issues in Criminology* 6, no. 2 (Summer 1971):76, 77; *Boston Pilot*, 25 July 1863; *Boston Herald*, 17 July 1863; Elizabeth Hafkin Pleck, *Black Migration and Poverty, Boston 1865–1900* (New York: 1979), pp. 23, 24.

6. Arthur Mann, *Yankee Reformers in the Urban Age* (Cambridge, Mass.: 1954), p. 41; James Jeffrey Roche, *Life of John Boyle O'Reilly, Together with His Complete Poems and Speeches* (New York: 1891), pp. 305, 306, 308; for dispute over the statue see this author's "The Crispus Attucks Monument Controversy of 1887," *Negro History Bulletin* 40 (January–February 1977):656, 657; also, "John Boyle O'Reilly—Apostle of

Racial Equality," *Boston Pilot*, 27 June 1975; for O'Reilly's days in Australia see Martin C. Carroll, *Behind the Lighthouse: The Australian Sojourn of John Boyle O'Reilly (1844–1890)* (Ann Arbor, Mich.: University Microfilms International, 1955).

7. John R. Betts, "The Negro and the New England Conscience in the Days of John Boyle O'Reilly," *Journal of Negro History* 51 (October 1966):249, 255, 256, 258; Roche, *Life of O'Reilly*, p. 288.

8. Roche, *Life of O'Reilly*, pp. 288, 348; Walsh, *A Newspaper for the Irish Immigrant*, p. 211; *Boston Pilot*, 28 June 1890.

9. Roche, *Life of O'Reilly*, pp. 353, 356, 359, 369.

10. Daniels, *In Freedom's Birthplace*, p. 229; *In Memoriam, Robert Morris, Sr., An Account of Funeral Obsequies and Memorial Meeting* (n.p.: 1882), pp. 5, 22, 34, 35; M. P. Curran, *Life of Patrick A. Collins, With Some of His Most Notable Public Addresses* (Norwood, Mass.: 1906), p. 12; Lord, Sexton, and Harrington, *History of the Archdiocese*, 2:611, 709, 3:17; Albert S. Foley, S.J., *Bishop Healy: Beloved Outcaste* (New York: 1954), pp. 7, 8, 66, 80, 81, 108–10. A collection of Bishop James Healy's sermons can be found in the Holy Cross College Archives, Worcester, Mass.

11. For Negroes in Catholic institutions see Journal of the Superintendent of the Home for Destitute Catholic Children, 17 June 1871, deposited at the Nazareth Child Care Center, Jamaica Plain, Mass., and *The Working Boy*, February 1904; Rev. Daniel T. McColgan, *A Century of Charity: The First One Hundred Years of the Society of St. Vincent de Paul in the United States*, 2 vols. (Milwaukee, Wis.: 1951), 1:336–38; William A. Leahy, "Archdiocese of Boston," in *History of the Catholic Church in the New England States*, ed. William Byrne, 2 vols. (Boston: 1899), 1:113, 114; Daniels, *In Freedom's Birthplace*, pp. 229–39.

12. Daniels, *In Freedom's Birthplace*, pp. 280, 281, 295, 296; *Boston Herald*, 4 December 1907; *The Boston Guardian*, 7 December 1907; Fitzgerald newspaper clippings, 23 April and 20 and 21 July 1910. Frequently undated and unidentified, the newspaper scrapbooks of John F. Fitzgerald are deposited at the Holy Cross College Archives (hereafter cited as F.N.C.). Herbert Marshall Zolot, *The Issue of Good Government and James Michael Curley: Curley and the Boston Scene from 1897–1918* (Ann Arbor, Mich.: University Microfilms International, 1975), p. 558.

13. Zolot, *The Issue of Good Government*, pp. 555–61; James Michael Curley, *I'd Do It Again: A Record of All My Uproarious Years* (Englewood Cliffs, N.J.: 1957), p. 154; *Boston Herald*, 14 February 1917; *Boston Globe*, 5 April 1915; Stephen R. Fox, *The Guardian of Boston: William Monroe Trotter* (New York: 1970), pp. 189–97; *Boston Post*, 11 and 22 April 1915; *Boston Guardian*, 7 December 1907; *Boston Sunday Post*, 18 April 1915; James Michael Curley newspaper clipping dated March 1917. Like the Fitzgerald collection many of the Curley newspaper clippings are undated and unidentified; they are deposited in scrapbooks at the Holy Cross College Archives (hereafter cited as C.N.C.); *Boston Post*, 22 April 1915; clipping from *Boston Journal*, dated August 1915, C.N.C.

14. Massachusetts Bureau of Statistics of Labor, *Census of the Commonwealth of Massachusetts, 1905*, 4 vols. (Boston: 1908–10), vol. 1, *Population and Social Statistics*, p. 368; John F. Stack, Jr., *International Conflict in an American City: Boston's Irish, Italians, and Jews, 1935–1944* (Westport, Conn.: 1979), pp. 23, 24. For background information on

the Jews in Boston, see Albert Ehrenfried, *A Chronicle of Boston Jewry From the Colonial Settlement to 1900* (n.p.: 1963) and Arnold A. Wieder, *The Early Jewish Community of Boston's North End* (Waltham, Mass.: 1962); Jacob Neusner, "The Rise of the Jewish Community of Boston, 1880–1914" (Honors thesis, Harvard University, April 1953), p. 130; Robert A. Woods, ed., *The City Wilderness* (Boston: 1898), p. 91; diary of Father Francis Casey, S.J., 21 May 1894, 10 April 1896, Jesuit Provincial House, Boston, Mass. For observations on Jews as real estate speculators see Woods, ed., *Americans in Process* (Boston: 1902), pp. 112, 113; *Boston Globe*, 6 July 1911; clippings dated 5 and 6 July 1911, F.N.C.; *Jewish Advocate*, 14 July 1911; clipping dated 7 July 1913, F.N.C.; *Boston Advocate*, 3 May 1907, 7 September 1906. Prior to 28 May 1909 the *Jewish Advocate* was known as the *Boston Advocate*.

15. *Boston Advocate*, 3 and 16 March, 4 and 11 May 1906, 20 September 1907; newspaper clippings, 18 January, 21 March, and 2 May 1916, C.N.C.; *Boston Advocate*, 29 June 1906, 22 and 8 December 1905; 6 April and 7 December 1906, 29 November 1907; Allon Gal, *Brandeis of Boston* (Cambridge, Mass.: 1979), pp. 85, 86, 90; *Proceedings of the School Committee of the City of Boston, 1905* (Boston: 1905), pp. 280, 336, 337, 431, 446, 447; *Boston Advocate*, 12 January, 30 March, 18 May and 22 June 1906.

16. Neusner, "Jewish Community of Boston," pp. 16, 58; *Boston Republic*, 1 January 1910; *Boston Advocate*, 9 June 1905; Frederick A. Bushee, "The Invading Host," in Woods, ed., *Americans in Process*, pp. 63, 64. For other comments on Jewish-Irish relations see Woods, ed., *City Wilderness*, pp. 134, 135; Rudolf Glanz, *Jew and Irish, Historic Group Relations and Immigration* (New York: 1966); Gal, *Brandeis*, pp. 78, 86, 89, 90; newspaper clipping, 25 November 1909, F.N.C.

17. Leslie G. Ainley, *Boston Mahatma* (Boston: 1949), pp. 4, 8, 21, 22, 45, 46, 55; *The Autobiography of Lincoln Steffens* (New York: 1931), pp. 615–27; Woods, ed., *Americans in Process*, pp. 173, 174.

18. *Boston Advocate*, 6 December 1907, 23 November 1906, 10 November 1905; *Jewish Advocate*, 1 July 1910; *Boston Journal*, 12 January 1913; Zolot, *The Issue of Good Government*, pp. 551–55; *Jewish Advocate*, 16 January 1914; *Boston Record*, 17 November 1917; *Jewish Advocate*, 9 October 1914; *Boston Journal* dated 1915 and January 1917, C.N.C.; Leonard Dinnerstein, "Atlanta in the Progressive Era: A Dreyfus Affair in Georgia," in *The Age of Industrialism in America*, ed. Frederic Cople Jaher (New York: 1968), pp. 138, 140, 141, 144, 145; *Boston Herald*, 7 February 1916; *Boston Journal*, 17 August 1916.

19. Stack, *Conflict in an American City*, p. 23; Massachusetts Bureau of Statistics of Labor, *Census of the Commonwealth of Massachusetts, 1905*, vol. 1, *Population and Social Statistics*, p. 368; Frederick A. Bushee, "Italian Immigrants in Boston," *Arena* 17 (April 1897):722–34; William Foote Whyte, "Race Conflicts in the North End of Boston," *New England Quarterly* 12 (December 1939):623–31; diary of Father Casey, 5 May 1895. For background information on the Italians, see Woods, ed., *The City Wilderness* and *Americans in Process;* William M. De Marco, *Ethnics and Enclaves: The Italian Settlement in the North End of Boston* (Ann Arbor, Mich.: University Microfilms International, 1980). For a later time period but relevant material see also Herbert J. Gans, *The Urban Villagers: Group and Class in the Life of Italian-Americans* (New York: 1962)

and William Foote Whyte, *Street Corner Society: The Social Structure of an Italian Slum* (Chicago, Ill.: 1943).

20. Lord, Sexton, and Harrington, *History of the Archdiocese*, 3:221–26; De Marco, *Ethnics and Enclaves*, pp. 88–91, 121, n. 9. For a good study of Irish-Italian conflict within the Catholic Church, see Silvano M. Tomasi's *Piety and Power: The Role of the Italian Parishes in the New York Metropolitan Area, 1880–1930* (New York: 1975).

21. Tomasi, *Piety and Power*, pp. 104, 105; Lord, Sexton, and Harrington, *History of the Archdiocese*, 3:222–27; Angelo Bonugli to Cardinal William Henry O'Connell, 19 September 1922, Sacred Heart Church of the North End folder, A.B.A.; Leahy, "Archdiocese of Boston," pp. 130–33; Gans, *Urban Villagers*, pp. 113, 237, 238. For a perceptive essay on Irish worship and parish organization, see Jay P. Dolan's *The Immigrant Church: New York's Irish and German Catholics, 1815–1865* (Baltimore, Md.: 1975), pp. 45–67.

22. *Report of the Catholic Immigration Bureau for the Year Ending March 24, 1912*; Augustine L. Rafter to Cardinal O'Connell, 5 January 1911; O'Connell to Rafter, 6 January 1911, 2 April 1913; O'Connell's secretary to Rafter, 17 April 1913, Catholic Immigration Bureau folder, A.B.A.; O'Connell's secretary to Rev. M. J. Splaine, 10 and 16 February 1915, J. C. Johnston to O'Connell, 28 June 1912, O'Connell to Johnston, 1 July 1912, Catholic Immigration Bureau folder.

23. Tomasi, *Piety and Power*, pp. 123–25; R. J. Haberlin to Father Sousa, 31 October 1918, Saint Leonard of Port Saint Maurice folder, A.B.A.; Reverend R. D'Alfonso to Cardinal's secretary, May 24, 1920; Vice-Chancellor to Father Raphael d'Alfonso, 26 May 1920, Sacred Heart Church of the North End folder, A.B.A.

24. Woods, ed., *Americans in Process*, pp. 118–20; *Boston Pilot*, 29 April 1876; *Boston Globe*, 10, 11, 12 and 13 March 1902; John Koren, "The Padrone System and Padrone Banks," U.S. Bureau of Labor, *Bulletin of the Department of Labor*, no. 9 (Washington, D.C.: March 1897), pp. 113–29; Edwin Fenton, "Immigrants and Unions, A Case Study: Italians and American Labor, 1870–1920" (Ph.D. diss., Harvard University, September 1957), 2 vols., 1:71–94, 144–46, 219, 220. By the 1920s the Irish held all but 55 of Boston's 347 union-elected offices. Stack, *Conflict in an American City*, p. 29. For Irish influence on the labor movement nationally see Warren R. Van Tine, *The Making of the Labor Bureaucrat: Union Leadership in the United States, 1870–1920* (Amherst, Mass.: 1973).

25. Fenton, "Italians and American Labor," 1:219–31.

26. Gustave R. Serino, "Italians in the Political Life of Boston: A Study of the Role of an Immigrant and Ethnic Group in the Political Life of an Urban Community" (Ph.D. diss., Harvard University, 1950), pp. 24–42, 56–59; newspaper clipping dated August 1911, F.N.C.; *Boston Republic*, 8 October 1910; *Boston Post*, 16 September 1917; *Boston Journal* dated 1915, C.N.C.; *Boston Journal*, 10 and 13 October 1917; *Boston Journal*, 1917, C.N.C.

27. Frederick A. Bushee, *Ethnic Factors in the Population of Boston* (New York: 1903, reprint edition, New York: 1970), pp. 151, 152. For background information on immigration restriction and post–Civil War American racial attitudes see Barbara M. Solomon, *Ancestors and Immigrants: A Changing New England Tradition* (Cambridge, Mass.: 1956), and John Higham, *Strangers in the Land: Patterns of American Nativism, 1860–1925* (New Brunswick, N.J.: 1955).

No Longer the Invading Horde

The Irish have easily amalgamated with our Americans.

President William Howard Taft in a Boston address, 1912

On an unseasonably warm evening in March 1912, more than 800 guests crowded into the main function room of the Hotel Somerset in the Back Bay to participate in the annual dinner of the Charitable Irish Society. Featuring a menu of oysters, brook trout, "Roast Jumbo Squab," and "fancy ice cream," and a head table graced by President William Howard Taft, Cardinal O'Connell, and Mayor Fitzgerald, the banquet was a long way from the days of the dreaded "coffin ships" that transported the ancestors of many of these very same guests from a famine-ravaged Ireland to Boston less than three-quarters of a century before.[1]

Thomas Ring, president of the Society of Saint Vincent de Paul, once observed: "Sometimes we are taunted with being the class that has the most of the poor. We admit the truth, while we object to the malice that prompted the remark." One had to go back, he maintained, "into the centuries of hate and persecution" to find "the real cause of the poverty that flooded this land with an immigration of poor unlettered people. But if we are told we throw our poor upon the community for support, let us say, we are part of that community and bear our share of that burden." The Irish did bear that burden, as evidenced by the matrix of charitable institutions and benevolent societies that they built and funded between 1845 and 1917.[2]

148

Often subjected to religious discrimination in the Protestant-controlled public school, the Irish furthermore would construct a parochial school system which, though less extensive than those of other Irish Catholic metropolises like Chicago, not only excelled in teaching the three Rs but succeeded in passing on the treasures of faith and culture. Thousands of unaccompanied women, pioneers in the truest sense, supported themselves and their loved ones back home by entering the demanding world of domestic service. At times treated unfairly, they courageously persisted, and by century's end, one could almost be certain that wherever upper-class Yankees were dining on codfish or scrod, it was being served by steady, dependable, female Irish hands. Beyond empirical measure were the contributions of wives and mothers, who stood guard over the fortunes of the Irish family.[3]

Although some managed to prosper as lawyers, doctors, journalists, and businessmen, the majority of Irish in 1917 still found themselves holding blue-collar or working-class jobs. What most hurt the Irish occupationally was not poverty, discrimination, or lack of educational opportunities but their uncommon success in politics and the labor movement. Although opportunities in business and the professions were available to those willing to take the risk, the Irish stranglehold over municipal jobs and other related patronage positions provided a security they would not sacrifice and inadvertently stifled the social aspirations of many Hibernians.

While Henry Adams retreated to his comfortable study to lament the demise of his homogeneous America, the Irish, facing the daily realities of living, working, and worshiping with minorities as different from themselves as Jews, Italians, and blacks, demonstrated that the melting pot could work. At the same time, they never lost sight of the fact that life was meant to be enjoyed, and they left a lasting impression on the worlds of professional sports and theater. Politics, Irish style, liberated Boston from the restraints of its Puritan past, as the Irish politician, ebullient and omnipresent, mingled with the populace at ward meetings, picnics, street-corner rallies, and neighborhood saloons.

NOTES

1. *Boston Globe*, 19 March 1912; Program of the Charitable Irish Society Dinner, 18 March 1912, deposited with the Stephen O'Meara Papers, Boston Public Library.

2. Ring letter dated 1892.

3. Mary Gove Smith, "Immigration as a Source of Supply for Domestic Workers," reprint from the *Federal Bulletin* 3 (April 1906) :1–6. Through one exchange agency alone, Boston Irish servant girls by 1880 were annually remitting $180,000 (Arnold Schrier, *Ireland and the American Emigration, 1850–1900* [New York: 1970 edition]), p. 107.

Afterword

The world has turned over a thousand times for the Boston Irish since 1917. In the aftermath of World War I, immigrant groups like the Irish were again threatened, as Protestant America, disillusioned by the peace settlement at Paris and labor unrest at home, insisted upon a return to Normalcy and One Hundred Percent Americanism. Immigration restriction laws, prohibition, the Red Scare, and the resurgence of the Ku Klux Klan all reflected a declining faith in America's ability to survive as a pluralistic society. The Irish strenuously opposed such reactionary policies and continued to defend the underdog by speaking out, for example, against the quota systems imposed on Jewish students seeking admission to Harvard University in the 1920s. Holding a virtual monopoly over city government, the Irish, despite complaints from other ethnic groups that they were discriminated against in the awarding of public works jobs, continued throughout the 1930s to function effectively in their historical role as pragmatic power brokers and as the "great amalgamator of race."

The Irish genius for reconciling differences between minorities was absent in post–World War II Boston. First, Boston was no longer a predominantly Irish city; the Irish who took part in the exodus to the suburbs were replaced by increasing numbers of blacks. In the 1960s, the power of Irish public officials was eclipsed when the federal government, responding to the civil rights movement, mandated affirmative action programs, quota systems, and eventually court-ordered busing as remedies for what many interpreted as wholesale discrimination against blacks and other minorities in employ-

151

ment, education, and housing. With America involved in the Vietnam War, the Boston Irish during the 1960s were additionally concerned with a Church struggling for relevance in a secular age and drastically altered by the leadership of Pope John XXIII and the decrees of Vatican II. As Vatican authorities were directing local pastors to celebrate Mass in English instead of Latin, church attendance dropped dramatically, many parochial schools closed overnight, and large numbers of nuns and priests sought release from their vows. Other issues, such as birth control, divorce, the right of the clergy to marry, and the right of women to become priests, added further controversy to the most calamitous decade in Boston Irish Catholic Church history. For those Irish who remained within the Church, the seventies brought further change when Humberto Medeiros, a native of the Azores, became the first non-Irish Archbishop of Boston in nearly 140 years.

The Irish began to move into white-collar positions as early as 1950. With more education and new opportunities in the fields of labor and administrative law, Irish attorneys, for example, made significant strides—a few even won access to the once-exclusive world of corporate law on Yankee State Street.

Enjoying new status and influence, the contemporary Irish American stands at a crossroads in his historical experience. Imperfect as they were, his ancestors did make lasting contributions to American politics and the labor movement. When government refused to act on behalf of the poor, sick, and unemployed, they had the political ingenuity and foresight to demonstrate that there was a legitimate role for the state in caring for those unable to fend for themselves. When there were few to speak for the rights of workers, it was the Irish who organized unions not only to protect their own interests but to save the free enterprise system from acquisitive, short-sighted capitalists. Facing an entirely different set of circumstances, the Irish of the 1980s must, as their fathers did, seek practical, nondoctrinaire solutions to new social problems, rather than make the tragic mistake of recent years—placing trust in social theories that reduce complex historical questions and circumstances to single causes such as race, sex, ethnicity, or class. Then, and only then, can America continue to move forward and to survive as a democracy and the last best hope on earth.

Notes on Key Sources

There are no easy ways to research the social history of the Irish in nineteenth-century Boston. Although somewhat outdated and at times judgmental, Oscar Handlin's *Boston's Immigrants, A Study in Acculturation*, rev. and enl. ed. (Cambridge, Mass.: 1959), is still the best overall study. Also rich in detail is Robert H. Lord, John E. Sexton, and Edward T. Harrington, *History of the Archdiocese of Boston*, 3 vols. (New York: 1944). The *Boston Pilot*, founded in 1829, touches upon many facets of Irish immigrant life. It was a lay newspaper for most of its existence until William Henry Cardinal O'Connell purchased it in 1908 and turned it into a diocesan weekly. More middle-class in orientation were the Irish weekly, the *Boston Republic* (1882–1926), and *Donahoe's Magazine* (1878–1908), a monthly.

The *Report of the Committee of Internal Health on the Asiatic Cholera* (Boston: 1849), Massachusetts State Library, State House, Boston, is a landmark document in the early Irish encounter with poverty. Nathan I. Huggins, *Protestants Against Poverty: Boston's Charities 1870–1900* (Westport, Conn.: 1971) provides useful information on the non-Irish response to poverty. Critical to the reconstruction of the Irish institutional response to poverty were the mountainous documents, reports, and correspondence pertaining to charitable institutions under the Catholic Church's auspices; these are deposited at the Archdiocese of Boston Archives, Brighton, Mass. Here, too, is the voluminous correspondence of William Cardinal O'Connell. Personal visits to several institutions led to the unearthing of additional primary materials such as the Journal of the Superintendent of the Home for Destitute Catholic

Children, deposited at the Nazareth Child Care Center, Jamaica Plain, Mass. The story of the gradual replacement of the volunteer charity worker by the professionally trained social worker is told in Roy Lubove, *The Professional Altruist: The Emergence of Social Work as a Career, 1880–1930* (Cambridge, Mass.: 1965). Thomas F. Ring (1842–98) was president of Boston's most active lay volunteer Catholic benevolent organization, the Society of Saint Vincent de Paul, and his papers and letters, deposited at the Society's headquarters in Boston, offer rare insight into Irish poverty and Catholic relationships with rival Protestant charitable agencies.

The pages of the *Pilot, Donahoe's Magazine*, and the *Sacred Heart Review* (1888–1918), a weekly written mostly by priests, contain innumerable scattered references to Irish women as young ladies, wives, and mothers and what was expected of them. These publications are deposited at the Saint John's Seminary Library, Brighton, Mass. The best introduction to domestic service, the occupation of many Boston Irish women, is David M. Katzman, *Seven Days a Week: Women and Domestic Service in Industrializing America* (New York: 1978). Some of the earliest indictments of Irish domestics can be found in a series of articles published in the *Boston Transcript* on 2, 4, 5, 7, 9, and 11 February 1852. In addition to the various annual reports of the Massachusetts Bureau of Statistics of Labor, the issues of the *Massachusetts Labor Bulletin*, and materials of the Domestic Reform League cited in the text, the logbook of the secretary of the Women's Educational and Industrial Union, deposited at its headquarters in Boston, is also useful in exploring the relationship between servants and the heads of household. In an interview with this author in 1976, the late Bridget T. Madden Burns kindly shared her remembrances as a Boston domestic.

Although prostitution was never a serious problem, the *Register, House of Industry, Deer Island*, deposited at the institution's office in Boston, does contain information on the number of Irish women incarcerated for this and other offenses. Comparisons between blacks and Irish in Elizabeth Hafkin Pleck's *Black Migration and Poverty, Boston 1865–1900* (New York:

1979) reveal data on Irish widows and the number of female-headed households. Newspaper clippings on the activities of suffragette Margaret Foley and the manuscript autobiography of Mary Kenney O'Sullivan, the labor leader, were consulted at the Schlesinger Library, Radcliffe College, Cambridge, Mass.

The recurring conflicts between Yankee Protestants and Irish Catholics over the public school in the nineteenth century are discussed fully and dispassionately in Lord, Sexton, and Harrington, *History of the Archdiocese*. How central the issue of social control was to proponents of the public school is revealed and discussed in the annual reports of the Boston School Committee and the Massachusetts Board of Education, and in Stanley K. Schultz's *The Culture Factory: Boston Public Schools, 1789–1860* (New York: 1973). In putting the development of the Boston parochial school system into national perspective, the author relied on James W. Sanders's splendid book, *The Education of an Urban Minority: Catholics in Chicago, 1833–1965* (New York: 1977). Differences of opinion within the Irish community on the wisdom of undertaking its own separate parochial school system can be found in the *Pilot*, *Donahoe's Magazine*, and the *Sacred Heart Review*.

The Sisters of Notre Dame de Namur are a teaching order which, from its earliest days, helped organize and staff many of Boston's parochial schools. The order's archives in Ipswich, Mass., contain a priceless assortment of school histories, attendance records, annals, memoirs, and even materials written by some of the students. The "Report of the Supervisor of Schools on First Official Visit, January, 1898 to January, 1899: Archdiocese of Boston Parochial Schools," deposited at the Archdiocesan Office of Catholic Schools, Boston, is indispensable to the understanding of the administrative growing pains of the parish school. Within its pages, Father Louis Walsh, the superintendent, offers a frank, firsthand assessment of prevailing conditions. Precisely what Irish children learned in the public and the parochial schools was ascertained by consulting the marvelous collection of primers and textbooks in the Monroe C. Gutman Library of the Graduate

School of Education, Harvard University, Cambridge, Mass. This material was augmented by the Golden Jubilee Books in the Notre Dame Archives and *The Working Boy*, a Catholic juvenile monthly, in the possession of officials at Saint John's Preparatory School, Danvers, Mass.

Information on student enrollment in the parochial school was obtained from the *Official Catholic Directory*, published annually since 1817 under an assortment of names. Other important statistics on the ethnic composition of public and parochial schools in Boston can be found in the United States Immigration Commission, *The Children of Immigrants in Schools*, vol. 2 (Washington, D.C.: 1911). The story of the Irish in higher education was pieced together by simply plowing through the many yearbooks, alumni reports, institutional histories, undergraduate magazines, student lecture notes, and faculty papers stored in the archives of Harvard University, Boston College, and Holy Cross College.

There is not a single good business history survey of nineteenth-century Boston; Justin Winsor, ed., *The Memorial History of Boston, 1630–1880*, 4 vols. (Boston: 1880–81), vol. 4, pp. 69–234, was of some use. Biographical background on Irish businessmen was derived from James Bernard Cullen, ed., *The Story of the Irish in Boston* (Boston: 1889, rev. ed. 1893), John J. Toomey and Edward P. B. Rankin, *History of South Boston* (Boston: 1901), Albert P. Langtry, ed., *Metropolitan Boston, A Modern History*, 5 vols. (New York: 1929), Richard Herndon, *Boston of Today: A Glance at its History and Characteristics* (Boston: 1892), and William T. Davis, ed., *The New England States*, 4 vols. (Boston: 1897).

No study of the Irish entrepreneur would be complete without referring to the credit ledgers of R. G. Dun & Company at the Baker Library, Manuscript Division and Archives, Harvard University Graduate School of Business Administration, Boston. Charles S. Damrell, *A Half Century of Boston's Building* (Boston: 1895), contains a smattering of information on Irish contractors, as does Sam B. Warner, Jr., *Streetcar Suburbs: The Process of Growth in Boston, 1870–1900* (Cambridge, Mass.: 1962). The reports of the Finance Commission of the City of Boston published in 1908 and 1909 expose the link between Irish contractors and elected public officials. Two helpful books on undertaking are Robert W. Habenstein and William M. Lamers, *The History of American Funeral Directing* (Milwaukee, Wis.: revised ed., 1962), and Curtis F. Callaway, *The Art of Funeral Directing: A Practical Manual on Modern Funeral Directing Methods* (Chicago, Ill.: 1928). The ledgers of undertaker John D. Fallon, in the possession of Ronald K. West, the proprietor of the Brady and Fallon Funeral Home of Jamaica Plain, Mass., give unique glimpses into the nature of an Irish undertaker's business and clients.

Good in their overall treatment of such questions as legal education, night school accreditation, admission to the bar, and selection of judges are James Willard Hurst, *The Growth of American Law: The Law Makers* (Boston: 1950) and Lawrence M. Friedman, *A History of American Law* (New York: 1973). A succinct essay on the history of law in the Bay State is Robert Grant's "Bench and Bar in Massachusetts (1889–1929)," in *Commonwealth History of Massachusetts*, ed. Albert Bushnell Hart, 5 vols. (New York: 1927–30), vol. 5, pp. 99–131. A composite portrait of the Boston Irish attorney and the type of law he practiced was drawn from Cullen's *The Story of the Irish in Boston*, William T. Davis, *Bench and Bar of the Commonwealth of Massachusetts*, 2 vols. (Boston: 1895), Conrad Reno, *Memoirs of the Judiciary and the Bar of New England for the Nineteenth Century*, 2 vols. (Boston: 1901), *General Alumni Catalogue of Boston University*, compiled by W. J. Maxwell (Boston: 1918), and the *Holy Cross Purple* and *Boston College Stylus*, student magazines, which periodically featured articles on the professional endeavors of alumni. Legal directories, pamphlets, and journals are deposited at the Social Law Library, Boston. One of the few book-length biographies on individual Irish attorneys is Katherine E. Conway and Mabel Ward Cameron, *Charles Francis Donnelly, A Memoir* (New York: 1909). The law folder and docket book of Joseph F. O'Connell, in author's possession, traced the steps of a young Irish lawyer in Boston in 1897.

Anyone interested in the history of medicine in Boston should first consult the massive holdings of the Francis A. Countway Library of Medicine, Boston Medical Library–Harvard Medical Library, Boston. One of the best monographs on the history of medicine, in terms of the profession itself and patient care, is Morris J. Vogel, *The Invention of the Modern Hospital: Boston 1870–1930* (Chicago: 1980). A profile of Boston's early Irish physicians was arrived at by consulting Cullen's *The Story of the Irish in Boston*, Thomas Francis Harrington, M.D., *The Harvard Medical School: A History, Narrative and Documentary*, 3 vols. (New York: 1905), and obituaries appearing in the *Boston Pilot* and *Boston Medical and Surgical Journal*. The only biography on a Boston Irish physician is *Michael Freebern Gavin, A Biography*, edited by his son (Cambridge, Mass.: 1915).

John E. Sexton and Arthur J. Riley, *History of Saint John's Seminary, Brighton* (Boston: 1945), is a thorough study of priestly training in the Archdiocese of Boston. Tracing the intellectual outlook of different generations of Boston's clergy is Donna Merwick's *Boston Priests, 1848–1910, A Study of Social and Intellectual Change* (Cambridge, Mass.: 1973). William Cardinal O'Connell left *Recollections of Seventy Years* (Boston: 1934), his autobiography, and Robert Aidan O'Leary's *William Henry Cardinal O'Connell: A Social and Intellectual Biography* (Ann Arbor, Mich.: University Microfilms International, 1980) is a balanced study of Boston's most illustrious and controversial prelate.

Journalism as a career attracted many Boston Irish. For biographical information on Irish journalists see Cullen's *The Story of the Irish in Boston*. For their contributions to one newspaper see Louis M. Lyons, *Newspaper Story: One Hundred Years of the Boston Globe* (Cambridge, Mass.: 1971). The *Pilot* was the principal organ of Irish opinion in Boston, and its history and the positions of its two most distinguished editors, Patrick Donahoe and John Boyle O'Reilly, on a multitude of social, economic, and racial issues are ably treated in Francis Robert Walsh's *The Boston Pilot: A Newspaper for the Irish Immigrant, 1829–1908* (Ann Arbor, Mich.: University Microfilms

International, 1969). The best biographies of O'Reilly and Donahoe are James Jeffrey Roche (a contemporary of O'Reilly), *Life of John Boyle O'Reilly, Together with His Complete Poems and Speeches* (New York: 1891), Francis G. McManamin, *The American Years of John Boyle O'Reilly, 1870–1890* (New York: 1976), and Mary Alphonsine Frawley, S.S.J., *Patrick Donahoe* (Washington, D.C.: 1946). Offering important data on the occupational standing of the Irish is Massachusetts Bureau of Statistics of Labor, *Census of the Commonwealth of Massachusetts, 1905*, 4 vols. (Boston: 1908–10), vol. 2, *Occupations and Defective Social and Physical Condition.* Stephan Thernstrom's *The Other Bostonians, Poverty and Progress in the American Metropolis 1880–1970* (Cambridge, Mass.: 1973) compares the social mobility of the Irish to that of the Yankees, Jews, Italians, and blacks. Of value in measuring the financial standing of individual Irishmen are the Suffolk County Probate Court Records, Boston, and the City of Boston Tax Assessor's Records stored at the Copley Square branch of the Boston Public Library.

To observe the Irish at leisure, one merely need consult the columns of the *Pilot, Boston Republic, Boston Globe*, or almost any other local newspaper. An intriguing book on the observance of death among the Irish is Seán O Súilleabháin, *Irish Wake Amusements* (Cork: 1967). John R. Betts, "John Boyle O'Reilly and the American Paideia," *Éire-Ireland* 2 (1967):36–52, chronicles the many activities of this avid outdoorsman and sportsman, while Betts's book, *America's Sporting Heritage, 1850–1950* (Reading, Mass.: 1974), views the nation's infatuation with fun and amusements. A good sketch of John L. Sullivan's boxing career can be found in William V. Shannon, *The American Irish* (New York: rev. ed. 1966), pp. 95–102.

The Music Department of the Boston Public Library has in its collection assorted materials pertaining to the colorful career of Patrick Sarsfield Gilmore, the famous bandmaster. One should read Carl Wittke's excellent article, "The Immigrant Theme on the American Stage," *Mississippi Valley Historical Review* 39 (September 1952):211–32, before consulting Harvard University's extensive holdings of playbills, books, and other miscellaneous items on the Irish on stage in Boston. Richard Stivers, *A Hair of the Dog: Irish Drinking and American Stereotype* (University Park, Pa.: 1976) offers some cultural and historical explanations of drinking among the Irish. Maurice Dinneen, *The Catholic Total Abstinence Movement in the Archdiocese of Boston* (Boston: 1908) describes local efforts to put an end to drinking among the Irish. Showing that the neighborhood saloon, as an institution, was more than just a place where the ordinary workingman went to quench his thirst is Jon M. Kingsdale's essay, "The 'Poor Man's Club': Social Functions of the Urban Working-Class Saloon," *American Quarterly* 25 (October 1973):472–89. How the Irish politician used the saloon institutionally to solidify his popularity and influence among his constituents is discussed in Robert A. Woods, ed., *The City Wilderness* (Boston: 1898) and *Americans in Process* (Boston: 1902).

By sifting through the innumerable volumes of newspaper clippings and scrapbooks at Holy Cross College Archives on James Michael Curley and John F. Fitzgerald, two of Boston's most flamboyant political figures, one can easily detect the Irish enthusiasm for the political rally and the campaign speech as art forms in themselves. Also useful in this regard are Curley's autobiography, *I'd Do It Again: A Record of All My Uproarious Years* (Englewood Cliffs, N.J.: 1957), Joseph F. Dinneen, *The Purple Shamrock: The Hon. James Michael Curley of Boston* (New York: 1949), Leslie G. Ainley, *Boston Mahatma* (Boston: 1949), and John Henry Cutler, *"Honey Fitz": Three Steps to the White House—The Life and Times of John F. (Honey Fitz) Fitzgerald* (Indianapolis, Ind.: 1962).

Because historians have focused almost exclusively on how the Irish related to the Yankees, we know little about Irish relations with blacks, Jews, Italians, and other groups. The standard work on blacks in Boston is John Daniels, *In Freedom's Birthplace: A Study of the Boston Negroes* (Boston, Mass.: 1914), while more recent ones are James Oliver Horton and Lois E. Horton, *Black Bostonians: Family Life and Community Struggle in the Antebellum North* (New York: 1979) and Elizabeth Hafkin Pleck, *Black Migration and Poverty, Boston*

1865–1900 (New York: 1979). John R. Betts, "The Negro and the New England Conscience in the Days of John Boyle O'Reilly," *Journal of Negro History* 51 (October 1966):246–61, explores the racial attitudes of one of Boston's foremost champions of racial and social justice. A first-rate history of the Jewish community in Boston has yet to be written. Of some assistance in examining the political relations between Jews and Irish are the several settlement house studies noted in the text, the Curley and Fitzgerald newspaper clippings at Holy Cross College Archives, and the *Jewish Advocate*, a newspaper on microfilm at the Boston Public Library. Herbert Marshall Zolot, *The Issue of Good Government and James Michael Curley: Curley and the Boston Scene from 1897–1918* (Ann Arbor, Mich.: University Microfilms International, 1975), contains important information on Irish political encounters not only with Jews but with other racial and ethnic groups. Ethnic tensions within the Catholic Church were not peculiar to Boston, as Jay P. Dolan and Silvano M. Tomasi have pointed out in their respective works, *The Immigrant Church: New York's Irish and German Catholics, 1815–1865* (Baltimore, Md.: 1975) and *Piety and Power: The Role of the Italian Parishes in the New York Metropolitan Area, 1880–1930* (New York: 1975). The problems of accommodation within the Church in Boston between the Irish, Italians and other ethnic groups are discussed in Lord, Sexton, and Harrington, *History of the Archdiocese.* By scrutinizing the descriptions of the different ethnic churches in William A. Leahy's "Archdiocese of Boston," in volume 1 of *History of the Catholic Church in the New England States,* ed. William Byrne (Boston: 1899), one can detect some of the nuances in religious expression characteristic of each particular immigrant group. Many ethnic parishes published their own individual histories, and other materials relating to the internal workings of specific ethnic churches can be located at the Archdiocese of Boston Archives.

Most studies of the Italians in Boston are sociological rather than historical in orientation. The padrone system and Italian involvement with Irish labor leaders in Boston are described in Edwin Fenton's "Immigrants and Unions, A Case Study:

Italians and American Labor, 1870–1920" (Ph.D. dissertation, Harvard University, September 1957). Information about their political contact with the Irish can be gleaned from the Curley and Fitzgerald newsclipping collections. Finally, the way the influx of these various ethnic groups caused Yankee Protestant leaders to question the democratic ideal of a pluralistic society is examined in Barbara M. Solomon's *Ancestors and Immigrants: A Changing New England Tradition* (Cambridge, Mass.: 1956).

Index